Praise for the First Edition

"Finally, a no-nonsense primer for leaders on how to build… and keep… extraordinary talent. This book should be in the briefcase of every exec in the world and should be pulled out every day for a refresher on how to be a *real* leader."

—**Dan Walker,** Former Chief Talent Officer for Apple, Inc.

"A fun and easy-to-read blueprint on understanding and creating engagement within a team. No high falootin' business jargon here—Martha Finney tells it like it is. She helps supervisors and managers uncover the secrets of employee engagement through behavioral examples, successes at top companies, and her charming storytelling."

—**Kirsten Clark,** Director of Global Workforce Training and Development, Save the Children,

"Martha succeeds in reducing one of the business world's most sought-after but amorphous concepts—employee engagement—into 69 digestible truths."

—**Christopher Rice,** President and CEO, BlessingWhite

"A must-read for new supervisors and managers, with lots of essential lessons and tips."

—**Tom Mathews,** Executive Vice President, Human Resources, Time Warner Cable

"Easy-to-read stories and useful truths about leading. I wish I had this book when I first became a manager. I had to learn some of these truths the hard way!"

—**Scott Shute,** Head of Global Customer Operations, LinkedIn

"The book is outstanding! Very easy to read… great examples, great advice, and the corporate world would be a better place if just 50 percent of the managers would follow your advice!"

—**Peg Wynn,** Former SVP/HR, Adobe

"I started reading and found myself grabbing for a highlighter. I got to the following line 'Getting the best is about building a culture of trust, connection, growth, and service.' I had to drop a box around that one."

—**Tiane Mitchell Gordon,** Senior Vice President, Office of Diversity and Inclusion, AOL

"Finney has gifted us an important compendium of accessible and eminently actionable insights about employee engagement. Using 'The Truths' as a guide, generations of managers will find infinite opportunities to unleash, inspire, and leverage the inherent talent in their people. My advice? Seize it! It will enable you to dramatically affect the future of your team, your organization, and your own career."

—**Jane Creech,** Founder and Principal, Strategic Business Systems (Organization Consulting and Leadership Coaching), Former Senior Director, OD, eBay

"If you are looking for a great way to deliver Management 101, just distribute this book. It has everything that someone new to management needs to know. Savvy, and sassy, and smart, this is an easy but important read!"

—**Beverly Kaye,** Coauthor, *Help Them Grow or Watch Them Go*

"Just when I thought one truth was as good as it could get, the rest lived up to it! I loved the anecdotes and the final truth, 'You're still the boss.'"

—**Ed Martin,** Chief HR Office, Pandora Internet Radio

"The subject is important, pragmatic advice told in an entertaining way. Front-line managers need this for perspective. This book has some great 'keys' to bringing out the best in people!"

—**Jim Wiggett,** President and CEO, Jackson Hole Group

THE TRUTH ABOUT

GETTING THE BEST FROM PEOPLE

THE TRUTH ABOUT

GETTING THE BEST FROM PEOPLE

Martha I. Finney

FT Press

FINANCIAL TIMES

Printed in the United States of America

First Printing December 2012

ISBN-10: 0-13-309518-5

ISBN-13: 978-0-13-309518-0

Pearson Education LTD.

Pearson Education Australia PTY, Limited.

Pearson Education Singapore, Pte. Ltd.

Pearson Education North Asia, Ltd.

Pearson Education Canada, Ltd.

Pearson Educatión de Mexico, S.A. de C.V.

Pearson Education—Japan

Pearson Education Malaysia, Pte. Ltd.

The Library of Congress cataloging-in-publication data is on file.

Vice President, Publisher
Tim Moore

Associate Publisher and Director of Marketing
Amy Neidlinger

Acquisitions Editor
Jeanne Glasser Levine

Editorial Assistant
Pamela Boland

Operations Specialist
Jodi Kemper

Marketing Manager
Megan Graue

Cover and Interior Designs
Stuart Jackman,
Dorling Kindersley

Design Manager
Sandra Schroeder

Managing Editor
Kristy Hart

Project Editor
Jovana San Nicolas-Shirley

Copy Editor
Keith Cline

Proofreader
Sarah Kearns

Senior Compositor
Gloria Schurick

Manufacturing Buyer
Dan Uhrig

All my thanks go to Colleen Cayes.
This book is for you.

CONTENTS

As a people leader, your job is simple: You are the link between organizational mission-critical objectives and the effort your employees invest in achieving those objectives. And you just have to keep those two pieces working together smoothly. See? Easy.

Yeah, right. As a people leader, your job is to inspire your employees to bring their personal greatness to work every day and to invest their best in your business. And that's a *hard* job. It's an emotional roller coaster. You experience the exquisite highs of engagement and teamwork when everyone is pulling together. Your heart breaks when you have to make really tough decisions that negatively affect the personal lives and well-being of people you truly care about. And it can be absolutely frightening when you're dealing with hair-trigger personalities who really don't belong in a safe workplace.

But even more routinely—and just as challenging, if not more so—you have to deal with yourself and your beliefs about life, about people, and about motivation and trust. Every day. Even on the ho-hum days. And that's when we get down to some pretty simple principles. Although this book by no means trivializes all the behaviors and beliefs that go into bringing out the greatness in your employees, the material you'll discover in these pages is based on a few very accessible assumptions:

■ **People leaders discover that leading is impossible when they forget that they're people first.** It may be paradoxical, but nothing makes a person come face to face with real—or perceived—limitations faster than a promotion into a managerial spot. On the outside, you may be projecting, "Can do!" (or at least hoping you are), but on the inside, you may be saying, "Uh oh, what have I gotten myself into?" Your first managerial assignment? Manage yourself into keeping in mind that you're not expected to be perfect. You're just expected to reach a little further for some brand new stretch goals.

■ **Most people want to do good work in a job they love.** Marketing consultant (and former Senior Vice President of Marketing for Starbucks) Scott Bedbury speaks about what he calls the "Five Human Truths." We need to be understood, feel special, feel as though we belong, feel that we're in control, and know that we have the chance to reach our potential. Although these feelings may not necessarily be what we want from a cup of coffee, they're certainly what we want almost universally from the work we do. (But ask me at 4 in the morning when I'm cranking against deadlines, and I might have a different answer for you.)

■ **Great people leaders don't have to be clever, complicated, politically astute, or even especially wise.** But they do have to be kind, honest, focused, positive, and authentic. If your company is committed to supporting you as you cultivate a grounded, authentic, compelling leadership style, you will see first-hand that creating great employees isn't about being magically charismatic. It's about being you.

■ **There is no *u* in team, but there should be.** As a people leader, you're also a team member. Sometimes you're the coach; in fact, you might often think of yourself in the top leadership spot. But you're also the water carrier. It's been said that great leaders are servants. And if your team is working so well and independently that all they need is a regular infusion of refreshment, that's a great position for you to play.

Enjoy this book. When you learn that creating great employees can be fun and personally rewarding, the first great employee you'll create will be yourself.

TRUTH

1

You don't need the carrot or the stick

Take a moment, if you will, to imagine the perfect day at work. By the time you arrive, everyone is already there. In fact, *you're* the last one to show up, and you're a half hour early! Other than the sound of fresh coffee brewing in the break room, the only other noise coming from that area is the sound of laughing as two coworkers share the fun of remembering the great day they had yesterday. Another conversation is focused on exploring ways that your team can put more quality, accuracy, functionality, and affordability into your flagship product that has already received every major industry award out there.

You sit down at your desk and log on. After a quick glance at the day's spreadsheet to confirm that all projects are ahead of schedule and on budget, you check your e-mail. You're thrilled to see your e-mail Inbox is crammed with messages from exuberant customers (many of the names you recognize from months and years of doing repeat business with them) thanking your department for yet another fantastic job. There are also at least 50 resumés there, all sent from your employees' friends who want to be considered for the next—rare—opening. And, look at that: an e-mail from the CEO letting you know that you're in line for this year's Chairman's Award for best performance in the company. Again!

> Engaged employees believe in the mission of their organization.

You look up from your monitor and around the room at everyone who works with you. You know something meaningful about every one of them. You're pretty sure by the way they're so dedicated to their work that each one of them must have read *What Color Is Your Parachute?*, done all the self-assessment exercises, and determined that their mission and purpose in life can be best fulfilled in *your* company, in *your* department. They all love their jobs. They are known these days as *engaged employees*.

Engaged employees are everywhere. And they have these general traits in common:

- Engaged employees believe in the mission of their organization.

- Engaged employees love what they do and understand how their jobs serve the bigger picture.

- Engaged employees don't need discipline; they need clarity, communication, and consistency.

- Engaged employees augment their skill sets with positive attitudes, focus, will, enthusiasm, creativity, and endurance.

- Engaged employees can be trusted, and they trust each other.

- Engaged employees respect their managers.

- Engaged employees know that their managers respect them.

- Engaged employees are a constant source of great new ideas.

- Engaged employees will give you their best.

Engaged employees are a manager's dream. Put them to work on a clearly defined mission or goal, and set them free to do what they do best. The hardest part for you is the possibility that you may have to change your mind about your own skills and assumptions as their leader. Engaged employees can smell stupid management tricks a mile away. And nothing will disengage them faster than the experience of being handled. They only need to be lead with inspiration.

> Engaged employees are a manager's dream.

Not everyone has the potential of being engaged, of course. Some people still just want to punch in, punch out, and cash their check. But don't assume you can tell which is which—especially if you've spent your past years driving poor performers. With most people, there's a little gem of engagement potential glowing deep inside. Find that gem, and lead with that. You could find yourself leading a transformed department—and even loving your own job more.

With engaged employees doing their work—and doing it exceedingly well—your biggest problem as manager might just end up being what to do with all that extra time.

TRUTH

2

You have direct
influence over your
employees' passion
quotient

Former President (and D-Day mastermind) Dwight D. Eisenhower once said, "Leadership is the art of getting someone else to do something you want done because *he* wants to do it."

When he gave this definition of *leadership*, the concept of employee engagement hadn't yet been coined. The more elementary idea of employee commitment hadn't been fully explored yet either. Still, linking organizational objectives with individual contributor desire is the core of employee engagement. It sets up an environment where you have self-motivated people personally taking on the responsibility of getting the job done. Some of those motivations may be personal. Others may be shared by the group. But still, the personal desire is what keeps everyone's focus trained on the same goal.

Unless you became extremely unlucky somewhere along the way, you probably will not have to convince your employees that they *want* to storm foreign beaches bristling with enemy machine gun nests. So, in comparison with what Eisenhower had to deal with, how hard can your own job be? For most of us, the challenge is knowing what steps to take to make our leadership roles maybe a little easier—certainly easier than the job Eisenhower had.

The first engagement hurdle that new managers have to clear is accepting in their own minds that the power and responsibility of team culture lie squarely with them the minute they accept the promotion above their coworkers. Your new role equips you with the gift of finally being able to create the kind of workplace community in which you would like to work yourself—which, in fact, you do. You work for your employees as much as, if not more than, they work for you. Once you accept this new assignment, the rest of your obligations as a highly effective, highly engaging leader can be broken down into these five steps, as identified by the U.K. research firm Institute of Employment Studies:

You work for your employees as much as, if not more than, they work for you.

1. **Build relationships.** The last several centuries of the workplace history have been a series of untethering: from the plow and cottage, from the mill, the time clock, from the cubicle, from the workplace altogether. Still, though, people need each other to get their work done. Relationships are the freeways along which information, ideas, and innovation zip. It's up to you to make sure that your team culture promotes free exchange and accountability through solid relationships among people who trust each other.

2. **Flatten hierarchy.** You hired people for their smarts; let them use their intelligence to make critical business decisions. Drive ownership for decisions and ideas down and throughout your entire organization. Because much of the work is accomplished through relationships anyway—irrespective of official chain of command or formally approved information pathways— why not leverage the individual initiative that's already there, harness it, and make it work for you?

3. **Set a direction.** Your people will know whether they're on the right track if you tell them where they're going. And, of course, why. Keep their attention focused on their objectives. Give them as much latitude as possible to figure out themselves how to achieve those goals. And then back off.

4. **Give them feedback as often as they want and need it.** As you'll see later in this book, the old tradition of annual performance reviews should be jettisoned in favor of customized feedback. In the most recent years, the commonly accepted wisdom has been that only younger generations want more frequent feedback because they're 1) used to one-on-one attention and 2) they're still in early career development phases and so are especially interested in making sure their work is building the future of their dreams. But, in fact, Baby Boomers are also interested in building their careers. Some of them are starting over, either because of financial realities stemming from a rock-bottom economy or because they are reinventing themselves, starting a whole new phase of life.

5. **Develop the team.** Team cohesiveness may be more important and longer lasting than your own tenure with the group. You could be transferred away from your team, as part of your own developmental program, with your team left intact to continue working together without your leadership. Consequently, the most valuable service you could provide your team is to equip them to carry on without you—as a cohesive team.

As Eisenhower had said, your role as a leader is to urge your people toward a shared objective because they want to do it. It's also your job to equip your people to work together as a team so that they can continue to want their goals, even when you're not there to micromanage. That's an engaged team.

TRUTH

3

You get the best by giving the best

Every year, the popular software company Intuit gives itself a massive performance review. While Intuit is also always interested in how it performs for its customers and its shareholders, the focus of this particular survey is how well it serves its employees. More than 60 questions are engineered to answer 1 core question: How well do we live up to our promise of providing the environment in which our employees can feel great about doing their absolute best work? Intuit wants to know how well it's doing *engaging* its employees.

Intuit has also been learning what it gets in return for giving its best. At Intuit, highly engaged employees are:

- 2 times as likely to be high-performing employees
- 7 times more likely to feel appreciated for what they do for the customers
- 10 times more likely to come forward with an innovative idea
- 1.5 times more likely to stay, even if they are offered a better job elsewhere

Even though Intuit is headquartered in Silicon Valley—famous for the many ways companies trick out their workplaces like playgrounds with free latte bars and gourmet restaurants—Intuit's leadership knows that getting the best from its employees isn't about the toys and the free eats. Getting the best is about building a culture of trust, connection, growth, and service. That culture is sustained and enlivened by its managers one person at a time, one interaction at a time. That's employee engagement.

There are two ways of looking at the relatively new field of employee engagement. There is the positive way. Then there is, of course, the negative way. Let's start with the negative way first.

> Getting the best is about building a culture of trust, connection, growth, and service.

Disengaged employees are destructively expensive to have on staff. In the United States alone, they cost as much as $350 billion in low productivity. Their attitude also poisons the day-to-day experience of working at your company, chasing away your best employees—not to mention your best customers.

Here's the good news: Companies with a highly engaged culture have shown consistent growth and profitability over recent years, while their low-engaged counterparts report declines in market performance. One study has shown that companies with 60-percent to 100-percent engaged employees report an average total shareholder return of 20.2 percent. But companies with less than 40-percent engagement show a –9.6-percent return.

When you do the cost/benefit analysis, employee engagement is so cheap, it's practically free. It can begin anywhere within the org chart. Certainly, the experts will correctly say that an engaged culture must be created at the very top as an essential value to have any chance of thriving organization-wide. But, in truth, the engaged culture lives and dies in the moment-to-moment decisions and behaviors of supervisors and managers. So it only stands to reason that engagement can be born anywhere inside the company.

According to the Hay Group, up to 35 percent of the difference in business results can be explained by the day-to-day differences in the workplace cultures created by managers. So you, as the manager, can make it happen for your department, no matter where you are inside your company. The payoff will be immediate—even immediately visible—and ultimately measurable.

Does this payoff mean you must bring in free donuts and fresh sushi every day? No. Do you need to allocate budget and space for a half-pipe for skateboard practice outside the break room? No. Does it mean that you have to show personal interest and concern in the well-being of each and every one of your employees as individuals? Yes—even on those days when you're so busy or preoccupied you'd rather just spring for that skateboard half-pipe.

> Employee engagement is so cheap, it's practically free.

If you're managing people, you're standing squarely on the intersection between corporate mission-critical objectives and the personal ambitions, passions, and drives of your employees. If there's going to be a 30-percent difference between your department and your colleagues' departments, you can either take the blame or take the credit.

The choice is entirely yours. And so is the power to make a real difference—one person at a time.

TRUTH

4

It's not money that motivates

Don't get the wrong idea. This truth doesn't let you off the hook for fairly compensating your employees for the work they do. (Anxiety and growing resentment that come from being broke can be *very* distracting.) You can adequately—even lavishly—pay your employees, but if you overlook one most essential engagement tool, this is what you'll get: Ho-hum workers driving around in expensive cars wondering how they can fill this odd, empty feeling inside.

People yearn for purpose—for doing something that's important, something that engages their full potential in a way that's meaningful beyond their personal bank accounts. And that makes your job as their manager a little harder. You may not have as much control over their compensation and benefits program as you might like to have. But you do have control over how inspired they are and how connected they feel to the mission their jobs serve.

It's not about the company. It's about what the company is doing to make the world a better place. This may seem like an overly romantic or grandiose stretch,

People yearn for purpose.

but, in truth, most people's standards are realistic and modest. Very few aspire to be the one to save the world from Evil Genius with his finger on the button. Most people want to feel that thanks to their efforts, the world is a little better off by nightfall than it was when the day started.

And the truth is, it is! You just have to help them figure out how what they do makes it happen that way. The first thing, though, is for you to understand how your company improves the world—and then how your job serves that mission. With precious few exceptions (drug dealers and professional assassins are the only two jobs that come to mind at the moment), every paying job improves the day (or the world) for someone else. This is because money is motivated to change hands for one or more of only three reasons:

■ To relieve pain

■ To restore hope

■ To bring beauty into the world

Once you've connected your own job to one or more of these reasons, your next job is to help your employees make this connection for themselves. And that's going to require some imagination.

It's easy to show a mason that he's doing more than just building a wall; he's making a cathedral. It's even easy to show a hospital janitor that he's doing more than just mopping the floor for the fortieth time that day; he's saving lives. But this same connection can be made to elevate the vision and attitudes of all employees, no matter what they do.

A music teacher looks out at a room full of snot-nosed kids and wonders if she can do it another day, another year. Mozart was once a snot-nosed kid. And look how well he turned out. More recently, a high-producing salesman who traveled the world marketing telecommunications systems for airports quit one day because he felt that he was born for greatness. Airport electronics just wasn't doing it for him. No one took a moment to help him see that his product helps loved ones fly to one another safely and that when a traveler collapses on a concourse from a coronary, the telecommunications system kicks in and consequently EMTs arrive in seconds, saving a precious life.

Motivation, for this salesman, was not about winning the game of making plan for the quarter. It was about making a positive difference in people's everyday lives, which was exactly what he was doing. His boss just didn't help him see it that way.

Motivation is about making a positive difference in people's everyday lives.

Every job carries with it myriad ways employees can relieve pain, restore hope, and bring beauty into the world. Helping your employees make the connection between their daily deliverable and enduring meaning may not be the easiest, most obvious conversation you can have. But, with a little one-on-one exploration, you'll find that connection together. It could be with the product itself, the customers themselves, the community, the coworkers, even the employee's family and the dream future your employee's job with your company is helping them realize.

And the conversation you have with your best employees exploring those ways is many times more pleasant than the one that begins with "Is there any way we can change your mind about leaving? More money, perhaps?"

TRUTH

5

Employee engagement isn't for sissies

It's easy to underestimate the full impact of employee engagement and how it's going to challenge you, not only as you implement it but also as it helps you carry your company's values into the future. In its simplest definition, you could say that employee engagement is about getting the absolute best effort from your employees by making them feel good about the work they do. What could be so bad (or hard) about that?

Employee engagement is not a namby-pamby trip to Candyland—just another employee commitment fad. Trivialize employee engagement and you're going to be playing the Hell edition of Twister. And that won't be any fun at all. Not one little bit.

If you take employee engagement seriously, you take on a no halfway, no turning-back high adventure of finding out just how far your personal and organizational courage will take you. Here's why you had better be really sure you want to do this:

> **Trivialize employee engagement, and you're going to be playing the Hell edition of Twister.**

- **Once you're in, there's no getting out.** If you're going to do engagement right, you must go public with your commitments to align your company's actions to its stated set of values and mission. Once you go public, you're stuck with your promise. If you ever withdrew that commitment, you would break valuable bonds of trust, and in the process rip out a lot of heart and talent. Recovery would be long and painful—if you could achieve it at all.

- **You have to be able to take a good hard look at yourself.** You can make a list of ideal values for your company, your department, and your own personal life as idly as leafing through an upmarket catalog. Everything looks so delightful and so within reach. But fantasy and real world collide when you tally the potential costs of every must-have. You have to decide what you can't live without and what is a luxury. Which values do you prize over all other values? Which would you quickly abandon when times got tough? Know the difference between the two sets, get real with yourself, and base your commitments on your limitations.

Which values do you prize over all other values?

- **You have to be prepared to choose passion over profit.** There will be times when the most expedient response to an issue is the one that will make you money. If that choice violates the engagement bond that you've established with your organization, you will start paying for that so-called profitable choice almost instantaneously as your actively disengaged employees rise up—or go underground, which could be even worse.

- **You can't finesse or ignore the numbers.** Companies that are serious about improving their culture will invest in high-quality, well-designed employee surveys. There will be numbers that relate directly to the way you manage your direct reports. When the scores come back, you have to face them head on and then let your people know exactly how you intend to improve your performance to serve them better.

- **You must be willing to cut loose the star players.** You will face some agonizing decisions as you move forward with your engagement initiative. One of those choices may be what to do with the bullies who are also the ones bringing in the big numbers. The star players who are the top performers in every one aspect of their jobs—except for the fact that they make life miserable for others—are more expensive than you can know. They cost the company in reputation as a best employer, and they chase away employees who know that they can do just as well elsewhere and be happier. They may even stain the company's external reputation by the way they treat customers and vendors. Getting rid of these people will be painful (especially regarding your department's performance), but keeping them will be even more painful.

- **You must be able to keep the faith over the din of the skeptics.** You've just given your starting lineup the boot. Your numbers are dipping (temporarily). Your quarterly report requires some explaining. The stockholders are becoming disenchanted with this whole engagement thing. You think, "If I hear the word *values* one more time, I'm going to quit." That's when you have to keep the faith and be willing to stand toe to toe with the skeptics (especially the one in the mirror) and remind them that no one said that engagement was going to be easy.

TRUTH

6

Real engagement gains happen after survey scores come in

If you didn't like getting report cards as a kid, it's a fair bet that you don't like facing the results of your company's engagement survey as an adult. It's only natural. Who likes to be scrutinized, measured, and reported on? No matter how professionally the survey is administered, it still feels as though you're under a spotlight—judged in very large part by the people who work for you. Depending on your company's policy regarding how the survey results are viewed over time, your own chances for promotion might get dinged if there are no signs of improvement year over year.

Try to forget about all that, if you can.

It's what you do with the survey results that makes the big difference in engagement gains over the period before the next survey is administered. That's almost completely within your control. First thing to do: Resist the urge to tuck the results report into the way-back of your hard drive, desk drawer, or truck bed. The survey isn't a test you pass or fail. It's a reflection of your team's current state of enthusiasm for their work and the workplace culture. Keeping that in mind might help keep you from taking it personally and from avoiding eye contact with your employees.

The survey isn't a test you pass or fail.

"Choosing not to do anything with the survey results is disengaging itself," says Jeffrey Jolton, director of consulting for Kenexa, a talent management and research firm. "How would you feel if I walked up to you and asked 'how are you?' and just as you start answering I turned around and walked away? I don't acknowledge you. I don't respond. It's going to leave you feeling empty, disconnected, and weird. That's what happens when you give a survey to your people but then don't follow up. When you leave your people hanging, it creates a distraction."

Managers let the months go by without settling down to address the survey results for a variety of reasons—none of them very good ones.

You don't see the survey as being relevant to what you're doing as a manager. This is especially true among managers who focus more on processes and parts than they do on people.

Dealing with survey results hasn't been modeled well by your superiors. It's natural to make priorities of those things that your own boss prioritizes. If your own survey about your manager has been swept under the rug, that's a strong cue to you that it's acceptable for you to do same. Don't.

Or you're concerned about dealing with your team's emotions and perceptions of what kind of leader you are. (Or maybe you're even afraid of your own emotions.)

Or you simply don't know how to work through the results with your team and take action on their comments. Jeff Jolton offers these suggestions:

- **Come to your team meeting undefensive, if you can.** "Managers are often afraid of the process, especially the first time through," he says. "But when I meet them afterward, they frequently tell me that it was one of the most engaging experiences for them personally. They'll realize that their team members actually want to help them, not work against them. In the ensuing months, they're much happier and their people are much happier."

- **If the survey results are truly abysmal and you think that the team meeting will escalate into an out-of-control complaint fest, arrange to have the team meet twice.** You're not there the first time. But someone everyone trusts is: a fellow team member with a leadership role, someone from HR, or even a professional mediator. Have them use that meeting to organize their thoughts, vent their emotions, and decide what they want to say to you for improvement expectations. You're present for the second meeting. And by that time, let's hope, everyone will be able to focus on improving team communication and processes moving forward.

- **Commit to making improvements only on one to four items for the upcoming year.** As a team, work together to select those items and describe what the improved scenario will look like. You don't have to promise the moon. And some improvements require cooperation up the org chart that you have no control over. Don't overwhelm yourself with across-the-board promises of improvements. That will set you up to fail.

■ **Call attention to the improvements as you make them.**
It might seem immodest to toot your leadership horn, but you
can't expect your team to notice the changes on their own. We're
not wired to notice the *absence* of pain. (When, for instance,
was the last time you noticed the instant an excruciating itch
disappeared?) Report back to your team that you took action on
their concerns. Or reference the survey conversation throughout
the year in other team meetings to let them know
you're still committed to those agreements you made.

TRUTH

7

Your behaviors are your brand

Brand experts will tell you that you build an enduring relationship with customers by connecting them emotionally with your product. Sure, it's essential to provide a product that is consistently excellent and priced to appeal to your customer base. But you also have to make them *feel good* about what you're selling.

As a manager, you have a brand, too. The way you treat your people categorizes you as a certain type of commodity among your most valued customers—your employees. Just like a box of soap or a cast member at Disneyland, your own features deliver hundreds, if not thousands, of touchpoints to your customers. These are moments of truth when your people experience your management brand promise and decide whether they're going to remain loyal customers. The way you treat your employees on a daily basis—even in those insignificant moments—makes up *your* brand promise. And it determines how much brand loyalty your people have to your company and to your department.

> The way you treat your employees on a daily basis makes up your brand promise.

Are you proud of your current brand promise? Or is it time for a major brand overhaul? The answers aren't necessarily easy or obvious. Just like there are many brands of soap and a wide selection of amusement parks to pick from, there is a variety of "right" management behaviors. They just have to be consistently appropriate to the culture you want to establish and the values you want to promote. Assuming you don't behave like a character out of a Charles Dickens novel (Scrooge, for instance), and assuming you behave like a basically decent human being, your management behavior brand can have a variety of characteristics and still be engaging. It just has to create the emotional experience you want your employees to have and, in turn, to provide to their customers.

> Your management behavior brand can have a variety of characteristics and still be engaging.

■ **Do your personal habits demonstrate quality standards you expect from your team?**

If you want a clean and organized department, how tidy is your own work area? If you need employees who speak well and correctly to your customers, does your grammar meet that same standard? What about your vocabulary? Do the words you use set the right tone of formality or informality that would make your customers feel at ease? Do you dress at least as well as you expect your customer-facing employees to dress, even if you sit behind a desk all day?

■ **Do you treat your employees the same way you expect them to treat their customers?**

If you want a high level of customer service coming from your department, you need to show a high level of customer service in the way you treat your employees. Do you return their phone calls and e-mails promptly? Do you honor your appointments with them? Do you keep their secrets? If a fleeting bad mood makes you edgy, do you take it out on your people, even if it's only just a little bit? Do you lightly shrug off the rare, innocent mistake? Or do you routinely overlook sloppy work? Or do you pounce on a slip-up as if it were a deadly virus about to be unleashed on Los Angeles?

■ **Do you fit into the overall company culture?**

You are your company's kind of manager if its customers are your kinds of people. Companies whose customers prefer a high-end, formal experience are best served by employees who behave in a high-end, formal way. And those employees are best served by managers with a more formal demeanor themselves. (The opposite is also true, of course. The waitstaff from Le Cirque would be *poissons* out of water at TGI Fridays.) What that means in specific terms, naturally, depends on the company itself. But if you're not feeling comfortable in the environment there, either internally or in the way the company faces its customers, it's possible that your own personality is a poor fit with the company's brand.

So the final question is this: Are you your company's kind of people? If not, you have two choices: change your branding behaviors, or change your company.

TRUTH

8

You can't give what you don't have

The heat is on. As companies are developing a growing awareness of the real bottom-line value of employee engagement, the pressure to create that relationship is put directly on the shoulders of front-line managers. And that's where it belongs. According to the Hay Group, as much as 30 percent difference in business performance can be attributed directly to the way managers treat employees. However, judging from the accountability that senior leadership places on managers to boost the engagement or satisfaction scores that come out of annual surveys, it would be natural for managers to feel at least 80 percent responsible for that difference in business performance. Engagement, no matter how satisfying it is, is a heavy burden for you to carry.

The question is this: Are you feeling that same level of engagement you're expecting to provide your employees? If companies aren't assuming responsibility for your needs as an employee, you're not a catalyst for high-performing, engaged cultures. You are the scapegoat for the failures of your senior management, who may want the benefits of engagement but not the hard work that goes into it. If you're not engaged yourself, you can't inspire your employees to any level of emotional dedication to their work.

Companies that measure engagement rely on a certain set of characteristics that describe the ideal experience their employees have on the job. Some start with an off-the-shelf product, such as Gallup's Q12

If you're not engaged yourself, you can't inspire your employees.

questionnaire. Others evolve their own custom list, usually with the help of consultants who specialize in engagement and surveys. No matter what the list is or how it's specifically worded, the items most commonly reflect some or all of the following sentiments:

- My company's values are similar to mine.
- I believe in my company's future.
- I see how my job serves the company's big-picture mission.
- I have what I need to get my job done.
- I have faith that the company can adapt to market changes.

- If I'm offered a comparable job at comparable pay, I'd choose to stay here.
- I'd recommend this company to all my friends.
- I happily go above and beyond the call of duty in my work.
- I know my boss cares about me, the work I do, and my professional future.

If your company performs an annual survey to measure employee engagement, those statements probably look at least somewhat familiar to you. But as an engaged manager of engaged employees, you have an additional set of needs and variables. Even though you might not see these statements on the survey, how would you answer them?

- My senior leadership stands by me, even when I have to make a tough people decision.
- My boss wholeheartedly believes in the mission of the company and how our department serves it.
- I have all the resources I need to attract and retain top talent.
- I respect and trust my boss.
- My boss respects and trusts me.
- My supervisor gives me the training I need to be a better people leader.
- My leadership knows that I'm trying hard and recognizes my efforts to improve as a manager.
- I believe in the initiatives I have to implement that directly affect my staff.

As a people manager, you deserve to experience all the same engagement characteristics that your employees do (and then some). You need the confidence and respect of all your coworkers—above you and below you on the org chart—to do your job brilliantly.

> You need the confidence and respect of all your coworkers to do your job brilliantly.

So if you're not feeling that you're getting the engagement support from your boss that you're expected to provide your direct reports, speak up! And preferably before survey season begins. Your initiative now will show up later in improved scores above you and below you.

But most importantly, performance and results will improve all around. And that, as a manager, is one of your chief responsibilities.

TRUTH

9

"Best" doesn't mean the same thing to everyone

It's easy—indeed trendy—to throw around words such as *best, breakthrough, knockout,* and *great* in business conversations. And, of course, we all know what those words mean generally. But what do they mean specifically to you? And, just as important, what do they mean to the person you're talking to? If you, your boss, and your employee have even slightly different interpretations of these words, those subtle shifts of meaning can confuse the way you assess the quality of performance and production.

You can't possibly know whether you *have* what you want until you know what you want in the first place. On an organizational level, companies find this out very quickly when they take on an engagement initiative and start asking themselves (and, hopefully, their employees) what *best* looks like in their company. And then they start spitting out engagement surveys. Many find that the famous—and ferociously copyrighted—Gallup Q12 set of questions is a good place to start. But then, as each department starts getting excited about the endeavor, it throws in more specific questions. And soon the survey is an out-of-control behemoth that measures nothing other than how many questions can get shoved into one questionnaire. (One company ended up with over 400 questions!) The result? Even after 400 questions, the company might still not know what *best* actually means in terms of behaviors and return on effort.

On an individual managerial level, you don't need 400 questions—or even 12—to help you refine your ideas of what a best employee is or to know when an employee is giving you her best. But you do need to know what *best* means

> It's a matter of fit of your employees' behaviors and characteristics with your expectations.

to you, the boss. Assuming that all the legal and moral issues are buttoned up, the definition of *best* is not a matter of right or wrong. It's a matter of fit of your employees' behaviors and characteristics with your expectations.

Start making a list of what constitutes best performance from all your employees. Don't automatically overlook the behaviors that you determine to be meaningless. Just as the white space in a painting is as important to the composition as the vase of pretty flowers is, you can learn as much about your values by what you don't care so much about as you do about what you do care about.

Are these best characteristics and behaviors in your book?

"My *best* employee…"

- Is dedicated to perfect attendance, no matter what.
- Is single-mindedly focused on the job at hand.
- Is passionate about understanding how each job in the department serves the company's larger mission.
- Is always optimistic.
- Is always skeptical.
- Freely offers advice, opinions, and ideas at all meetings.
- Is reliably devoted to process and rules.
- Is always looking for a new and better way of solving old problems.
- Bends over backward to serve the customer.
- Values process efficiencies and scalability.

These are just a few characteristics that have been identified as best behaviors of high-quality employees, and you'll see that some contradict each other. Each one has benefits but also disadvantages. You may agree with some; you might find others absurd. Remember, there is no right and wrong. It's only about fit.

Your own list will grow as you learn more about yourself and what works within your department and company. Discern which are your preferred behaviors, and you'll know when you're getting what you want in your department. Then you'll be able to lead your staff with reassuring clarity and consistency.

> There is no right and wrong. It's only about fit.

But you're not done yet. You have a boss as well, with his or her own ideas of what constitutes *best*. After you've had the chance to develop your list to the point where you decide it is comprehensive enough to cover most expected behaviors and characteristics in your department, review it with your boss to see if you two agree.

The point here isn't to give your boss the opportunity to tell you how wonderful you are. Your purpose is to make sure you share the same values and expectations as your team. That would be the best thing.

TRUTH

10

Think you're a great leader? Think again

The scene is so famous that all we have to do is mention the title of the movie to know exactly what we're talking about: *When Harry Met Sally*. In case you're not a moviegoer, there's the setup. Harry and Sally are sitting in a New York diner comparing his perceived track record of excellent, um, performance against general demographic statistics that reflect an overall dissatisfaction among women. His point: Yes, but I'm different. Her point: Every man thinks he's an exception to the statistics. And then she says, "You do the math."

Workplace math is showing a similar disconnect between perception and reality. A study reported in late 2006 showed that 92 percent of managers say that they're doing an "excellent" or "good" job managing employees. But only 67 percent of the employees agree. An additional 10 percent say that their bosses are doing a "poor" job. As Sally said, "You do the math."

In a separate survey that has been tracking employees' overall esteem for their executive teams, there has been a noticeable decline in the employees' respect and trust that their management is making

> Workplace math is showing a similar disconnect between perception and reality.

decisions that will ultimately result in a healthy and competitive company. Only 49 percent of employees say that they have "trust and confidence" in their managers' performance—down from 51 percent a few years earlier. Employees are also reporting less confidence that their managers are behaving and making choices that reflect the company's core values.

Could you be a Harry, blissfully moving through your workdays assuming that all your employees are fulfilled and satisfied with their jobs? If you're assuming that you can *just tell* that your employees are satisfied by the way they behave in front of you, you could be putting valuable relationships at risk.

There are ways you can close the perception/reality gap. If you're fortunate, your company already administers 360-degree performance reviews, in which your own performance is being rated not only by your boss but also by your direct reports. As hard as it may be to stand under such bright scrutiny, swallow your pride, submit, and then pay very close attention to the feedback you get from everyone who works with you.

But even if your company doesn't invest in such formal surveys, you can always do a little investigation of your own. You can go the direct route and ask your employees this excruciatingly humiliating question: Am I as good for you as I am for me? But don't expect a straight answer. (It didn't work for Harry, so it probably won't work for you.)

Or you can keep a self-diagnostic test running consistently in the back of your mind as you move through the day:

- Do I make sure my employees know how their jobs are tied to the organization's overall strategy?

- Do I make a point of keeping them informed on all news and changes affecting the company and their jobs as soon as possible?

- Do I get back to them immediately when they're waiting for a decision from me that affects their own lives—such as vacation leave requests and promotions?

- Do all my actions reflect and support the company's values?

- Do my behaviors set the example for the kind of healthy, collaborative culture I want to establish in my group?

- Do I keep their personal issues confidential?

- Do I speak positively about them to their coworkers?

> Do my behaviors set the example for the kind of healthy, collaborative culture I want to establish in my group?

- Do I pay attention to each of my employees individually, demonstrating to them that I care about their personal and professional development?

- Do I take all the necessary actions to show my employees—both as a group and as individuals—that I appreciate all that they are doing for our department and the company as a whole?

- Do I keep my promises to my employees?

Statistics show that when employees quit their jobs, it's most often because they are dissatisfied with their direct supervisors. While you can't force an employee to stay with you, you can certainly give your employees every reason to want to stay.

Close the perception/reality gap about the quality of your own performance, and your employees won't be tempted to look to other employers and say to themselves, "I'll work where she's working."

TRUTH

11

You could be your own worst employee

By the time most of us reach the place in our careers where we have the privilege of managing other people, we have already been subject to a variety of management styles. Few of us are lucky enough to have worked only for inspired, inspiring, wise, mentally healthy supervisors. Maybe your first "supervisor" was an overly strict parent who made you feel defensive and judged at every turn. Or maybe an early boss felt that his duty was to put you through the school of hard knocks—you know, toughen you up a little bit. Or maybe there's a boss in your past who followed every new management fad, only to drop it abruptly when the strain of upholding the fad's principles became too hard.

None of us can expect to go through an entire career completely unscarred by bosses' misguided behaviors and assumptions. If you've been supremely observant, you've probably developed a long list of "don't do's" as you've witnessed (or experienced directly) how disengaging some boss behaviors can be. But still, you're only human, and you probably absorbed some wrong lessons along the way. As a result, you have likely picked up some limiting beliefs about people.

You don't have to be a psychoanalyst to know when your beliefs are getting in your way. Watch the way your employees behave around you. There's high turnover. Your meetings are stonily silent rather than wildly collaborative free-for-alls. You keep facing the same types of problems, even though

The worst performer on your team could be you.

the employees are different. Your department is infused with worry, distrust, politics, and turf battles. You find that you have to do an inordinate amount of micromanagement and coaching.

The worst performer on your team could be you. If any of the following beliefs sound familiar, you may be unconsciously letting them drive the way you treat your people:

■ **They'll get over it.**

Seemingly insignificant, fleeting moments—like coming to work irritable one day and not saying good morning—can have lasting consequences. A grumpy mumble from you could be nothing more than just pre-coffee crankiness, but it could signal to your employees that their job is at risk. An overreaction? Probably. But even if it is, they won't just "get over it." Not, that is, until you take a moment to clean it up. Apologize.

- **My team is here to make me look good.**

  As true as that principle may be, that belief will make you a terrible leader. Turn that belief around and remind yourself that you're there to make *your team* look good. Take care of your employees, and you'll inspire trust, innovation, confidence, and above-and-beyond-the-call-of-duty dedication among all your employees. And that will, ultimately, make you look very good.

- **I'm not a bully; I just believe that tough love works best.**

  When did tough love actually work with you—other than scare you into action and make you think that your boss was an arrogant, cruel, mind-bending jackass? Your job isn't to love your employees, either tough love or real love. Your mission is to lead your employees and inspire them to love *their* jobs, but not at the cost of their peace of mind.

- **If the idea was any good, someone would have already thought of it.**

  In truly engaged teams, members can come forward with new ideas for doing a job better or providing better customer service or engineering a new breakthrough product. Maybe someone already did think of the idea before but was afraid to bring it forward to your predecessor. Or maybe the idea's first iteration was proposed at the wrong time—but now the market has changed and there's more money for research and development. Times change. Even old ideas have the chance to take on a fresh life. Welcome all ideas uncritically. That new Big Idea would actually be an old one whose time has come, coming from your department of creative geniuses.

- **I didn't have it perfect as I was coming up. If my employees don't like the way I treat them, they can just quit. They're easy to replace.**

  You're even easier to replace. Companies are getting better at releasing supervisors who won't release their past beliefs to grow into better managers.

TRUTH

12

Visionary or beat cop?
Your choice

The big business news that hits the headlines these days seems to fall into one of two large categories: Why didn't I think of that? and What were they thinking? The first leads to accolades and keynote speeches; the second leads to handcuffs and legal fees. One is good; the other is bad. But both reflect a need for two separate kinds of management styles: visionary and beat cop. Visionary managers may get the limelight because of their fascination with the power of possibilities. But if you're more enchanted with the power of rules, there's a huge demand for you, too. (Case in point: A Google search for Dodd-Frank pulls up almost 19 million hits. People are worried about following the rules.) The beat cop's job isn't a glamorous one with high visibility. And you probably don't want all that attention anyway. For a beat cop, a day without having to bravely smile into a phalanx of flashbulbs outside a courthouse is definitely a good day.

Growing up, we tend to know intuitively whether we're primarily visionaries or beat cops (although, as second graders, we probably talked more about whether we colored inside or outside the lines than our leadership styles). As adults, we grow up to be varying combinations of both. So we shouldn't claim to reside fully in one category versus the other, even though we still have dominant strengths and tendencies. When we become managers, we can use that dominant strength to do our best good for the departments and functions we serve. We will know what to expect from ourselves. And so will our people.

> We tend to know intuitively whether we're primarily visionaries or beat cops.

Here are some distinctions (generally speaking, of course) to differentiate visionaries from beat cops:

- Visionaries break new ground. Beat cops avoid breaking rules.
- Visionaries embrace inspiring scenarios. Beat cops prevent dire scenarios.

- Visionaries marshal strengths. Beat cops mitigate weaknesses.

- Visionaries prefer loose reins. Beat cops prefer more control.

- Visionaries need a sketchpad. Beat cops would rather have the rulebook.

It may be most fashionable these days to be a visionary. But the daily realities of business—in even the most innovative of industries—still require great beat cops who know the rules cold. They see their people as human beings who work hard to pay their mortgages on time and who would be very happy to stay out of jail, thank you very much.

And there's still a tremendous amount of room for creativity and innovation as a beat cop. Great beat cops know that they must have the power of relationships, trust, intuition, and inspired hunches to make sure that this day turns out to be a good day. While a visionary's career can be jet-propelled by the power of only one idea, the beat cop's success is measured by a track record of daily, monthly, and yearly dependable deliverables in a peaceful "neighborhood" of everyday people who know him well because he's out there walking among them.

That's a mission that takes a tremendous amount of vision. If you're more of a beat cop at heart, take pride in that role. Read up on the rules. And invest in a good pair of walking shoes.

TRUTH

13

Your health may
be compromising
your leadership
effectiveness

Put yourself in this hypothetical situation for just a minute. You're considering two excellent candidates for a critical job opening. They're equally qualified, brilliantly talented. Only here's the problem: One is in top shape. The other is straining at the buttons. Just the exertion of sitting down causes Candidate 2 to break a sweat.

Come on, tell the truth. You'd pick Candidate 1, wouldn't you? No one wants to discriminate, of course. But all else being equal, a solid business argument can be made for choosing the seemingly healthier one. You could possibly be wrong, but you might be able to point to lower predicted healthcare costs as a really good reason to be selective about who you bring on to the team.

There's also the unfortunate possibility that your team will discriminate against a fat new employee. In a study conducted by the University of Manchester and Monash University, Melbourne, researchers found that obese candidates are more likely to be discriminated against in the workplace than their more slender counterparts (in the case of this particular study, themselves after bariatric surgery). From a management perspective, wouldn't you want to hire the person most likely to hit the ground running (so to speak)—the one who will fit easily into the group?

Leadership potential was one of the selection criteria. And, because you're a manager, this is where you come in. What if you're obese yourself? Other unhealthful habits can also diminish your abilities to inspire and lead. Maybe you smoke? Or you come back from lunch with alcohol on your breath? If your employees are likely to give

> If you have been letting yourself go, your people will talk.

in to their human nature and discriminate against their unhealthy coworkers (even if only just a little bit and they hate themselves while doing it), how effective is their working relationship with, say, you?

If you have been letting yourself go, your people will talk. And they'll worry. According to a nationwide telephone survey conducted by the management consulting firm Healthy Companies International, 17 percent of the respondents reported that they were "at least somewhat worried" about their boss's health in the past year. And 4 percent said that they were very worried.

"Everyone's health is essential to top performance, including the boss's," says Stephen Parker, Health Companies International president. "For the entire organization to function well, no one's physical or emotional fitness can be ignored. With all that companies have to deal with—a fast-changing competitive environment, aggressive sales targets, or maybe a shaky business strategy—it's disturbing to learn that employees also have to worry about their superior's health."

If you have been letting yourself go, your people will talk.

It's so easy to assume that if no one is saying anything to you, your health issues aren't obvious. Don't kid yourself. People have noticed that you've put on a few pounds. Or you haven't been sleeping well. Or you've lost muscle tone. Or the color in your skin is off. You notice these things in others. And chances are that you might have mentioned your observations to trusted friends and colleagues, who will look too (now that you mention it) and agree. And speculate. Never harshly judging, of course. Always kind concern. But do you really want your team to be spending their time, energy, and focus talking to each other about what the deal is with you? Or do you want them focusing on their work?

As a leader, you're modeling more than performance standards for the work put to your team by the corporate objectives your group has agreed to take on. You're modeling your priorities and self-care behaviors that will show your team that you want them to take care of themselves as well. While some might say that healthful lifestyle habits should be out of your sphere of influence as a manager, Parker disagrees:

In increasingly stressful times, it's essential to develop a life and work plan that optimizes health, manages stress, and balances work, family, and personal life. Only in this way may one develop the resilience necessary to bounce back from setbacks and adversity.

You know what that means? Healthful eating at work. Daily exercise. The doctor appointments for checkups, and then the necessary follow-ups. The regular vacations where you can truly clock out and be with your family—a total getaway from work. And you honor the rights of your direct reports to do the same things.

Then one of these days, when people gather to talk about you, it won't be, "Did you notice those extra pounds?" It will be to tell stories of how you "took one for the team." By which they'll be meaning a healthful walk at lunchtime. Not that extra piece of cake.

TRUTH

14

You don't have to be perfect

The old saw goes like this: If you're not learning, you're not growing. The other saw goes like this: If you don't screw up now and then, you're not learning. So, collapse the two, and this is what you get: Screw up, learn, grow. Repeat.

That's a mighty big saw to swallow when you're the manager. Aren't you supposed to be a role model? Yes. You're supposed to be the role model of learning from your mistake and then growing from it.

> You're supposed to be the role model of learning from your mistake and then growing from it.

If you're managing people in a company that's serious about cultivating an engaged workplace, you're going to be expected to develop your own ways of keeping your employees passionate and excited about the work they do. And you're going to make a mistake now and then. The engagement-specific blunders that you'll make won't be technical; they'll be behavioral. Those mistakes are harder to measure. (You always know if you made deadline or plan, but are you really sure you didn't just hurt your assistant's feelings?)

This should make you feel better: Top leaders who are sincerely committed to creating engaged workplace cultures are also sincerely interested in your engagement. And they know that it's a never-ending learning process up and down org chart. People don't expect you to be perfect; they just want you to learn from the last time that you weren't. You build your power as a leader with your ability to say "I'm sorry."

> You build your power as a leader with your ability to say "I'm sorry."

Some companies that conduct annual engagement surveys offer their managers post-survey coaching and suggested action plans to improve those weaknesses that alienate their employees. Some even require you to post your new resolutions online so the entire company knows your plan. You know that dream where you suddenly discover that you're naked? It's sort of like that.

Maybe your company doesn't even have an engagement survey process. You can still work on your people skills. Your task is to be clear yourself on what your issues are and then make it clear to your employees that you "get it" and are working on them.

Hold a departmental meeting to go over your employees' issues as a group. Make the meeting as congenial as possible, putting yourself in the hot seat and reassuring your employees that you're there to learn from them.

Make their comfort with the process paramount. That way you'll get honest feedback. Never, for instance, make a single employee feel busted for making a complaint. If you want to see a resignation letter really fast, begin your meeting with, "Aw, c'mon, let's get real here. I know it was you who…." That, by the way, could also generate a termination letter. Yours. Just wait a day or two.

Let everyone in your group know that you sincerely want to improve the way you do your job and that you welcome everyone's thoughts. Set this up as, in effect, a reverse performance appraisal meeting, in which your direct reports can discuss your performance and then provide a clear picture of how you can improve the way you do your job.

Calmly ask questions that will help both you and your employees understand their own feelings about the issue. Before they've had this chance to talk it out—that is, not behind your back—the issues may have gotten so emotionalized that your employees forgot exactly what started bothering them in the first place.

Conclude the meeting with some agreements on changes you can make—preferably a few that you can measure. If one of the complaints is, for instance, "You never let us know what's going on," accept the objection evenly (forcing yourself to swallow any "yeah, buts" that are screaming to be let out of your mouth), and own the responsibility of keeping them more informed. Then together decide on a plan on what you can reasonably do to keep them in the loop. Perhaps you and your team can agree on a Monday morning weekly kickoff meeting. Or maybe they'll be happy with a weekly e-mail.

The main point of these meetings is to let your employees know that your number-one role as their manager is to help them do their jobs better. The more you give yourself permission to

Your number-one role as their manager is to help them do their jobs better.

be imperfect, the more these meetings will conclude with everyone thinking the same thing: "Phew! That was easy."

15

Your career can recover from an engagement hit

The success record of your career path over time is tracked in two ways. The first is your resumé. The second is your reputation. Although it's definitely not advised to fake your resumé, it's done all the time. Even famously. And those who are found out seem to be tripped up for only a split second. Then they move on.

It's not so easy to fake your reputation. When you screw up in a big way as a manager, word is going to get around. Let's face it. People like to talk. And they especially like to forewarn. So when people say, "Your reputation precedes you," they're not kidding.

But you're also human. So you're going to make leadership mistakes. When you're a manager, you are on a steep learning curve that never seems to end. The higher up you go, the more you'll have people at the receiving end of the consequences of your errors. And those people will talk.

Can you ever recover? Yes. (While this book was being written, a high-profile CEO resigned after it was revealed that he lied on his resumé. Was his future ruined? Seems not. He was named CEO of another high-profile company the same week his replacement in the previous company was announced. If he can bounce back, surely the odds are in your favor. I mean, really, how bad can it be?)

You *can* survive a star-crossed incident where you violated an engagement value that's cherished by your people. You will need to handle the upcoming months, even years, very carefully, though. That will give your track record of trustworthiness the chance to overrun and outlast the regrettable glitch. Fortunately, the most powerful things that you can do over that time take little energy, cost nothing, and have amazing impact.

> The most powerful things that you can do… take little energy, cost nothing, and have amazing impact.

"If you have a damaged reputation and people have suspicions about you, the most effective way to disarm any negative expectations that people will have about you is to be viewed as an absolutely fabulous listener," says Ian Ziskin, executive coach and president of EXec EXcel Group, a NYC-based talent management consulting firm.

"Be a good listener and look for opportunities to address some of the things that you hear about. Your track record for listening to your people and removing their roadblocks will soon be the word that gets around."

This is not about buying votes through good works. You are actively demonstrating your commitment to restoring a tightly woven fabric of trust in your time and reliability in your personal brand as leader.

Here's how you can shore up that slightly eroded trust: With your team, identify two or three critical initiatives that the entire group can take on over the next 6 months. Give them something they can focus on that will give them immense satisfaction as a group and that they must depend on each other—as well as you—to achieve. This way you are restoring a culture of team mutual dependability, while you're giving them something more satisfying and forward moving to concentrate on.

While your team selects and focuses on goals that can be achieved only when the entire group (including you) works together, also commit to personal development goals with each one of your employees. At least once a quarter, hold one-on-one meetings with your direct reports to explore and agree on what skill development goals they can work to achieve over the next 3 months. Increasingly, engagement research is showing that individual contributors recognize that they are solely responsible for their careers and future. So your people are more focused on how their hours at work are building their prospects than they are on that thing you did to violate their trust.

As you grow in your own career, you will have errors in judgment. (If you're not making mistakes now and then, you're not growing.) Your heart will have been in the right place, and it will have been an innocent mistake. But as much as it will be a learning experience for you, it won't be a mere classroom exercise for your people. It will affect your people in very real ways.

You'll just have to let the passage of time and the accumulation of positive events swing your career narrative away from the dings and toward a legacy of true engagement.

TRUTH

16

Employee happiness is serious business

Is it really your job as a manager to worry about whether employees are happy? No, not if you care only about bodies showing up and just pushing buttons and levers all day without any special thought about quality or safety. In that case, their happiness is irrelevant (to you). If your high turnover is acceptable, employee happiness isn't essential. If you can tolerate vandalism or workplace violence, go ahead and skip this truth.

Let's say, however, you'd prefer a workplace where people get along, voluntarily help each other, think independently and creatively, take safety practices personally, show up dependably, and take pride in the company they work for. In that case, employee happiness is essential. Employee happiness isn't a nice-to-do. It's a must-do. Here's why.

Barbara Fredrickson, University of North Carolina professor of psychology, has shown that emotions associated with happiness actually *expand* a person's ability to respond positively

> Employee happiness isn't a nice-to-do. It's a must-do.

to stresses of everyday life. Negative emotions, in contrast, narrow a person's "thought-action repertoire" to one simple thought: "Gee, I'd like to survive this bad moment" and the accompanying action, which is to skedaddle (or preempt anticipated violence with real violence of one's own). But positive emotions offer what Fredrickson calls the *broaden-and-build* ability to think creatively and use a variety of resources to cope with the moment.

Suppose, for instance, that an employee is facing down a mountain lion (or has spotted you heading straight for her cubicle). She first must decide what her chances of surviving this encounter are going to be. If she's steeped in negative emotions, there's going to be only one set of responses, gathered under the general category of *run (or fight) for your life!* If her emotions are generally positive, she might say instead, "I just love this job. The report's already on your desk. Let's grab some coffee so we can talk about opening that new market I was telling you about." Happiness expands your employees' options.

Fredrickson identifies three general categories of emotional states that spark happiness. Even though they're typically personal, they also have a direct impact on the workplace:

- **Joy.** We experience joy when we're feeling safe and that we're moving closer to our goals. Joy prompts us to feel playful and experiment with new ideas

Happiness expands your employees' options.

and skills. Joy also encourages us to be more social, which in turn helps us build healthy relationships. Joy makes us physically, intellectually, and socially more powerful to contribute to the world around us.

- **Interest.** Interest sparks curiosity, wonder, excitement, intrinsic motivation, and "flow" that sense of being thoroughly absorbed in a pleasurable activity. It also prompts people to build their resources simply because they, well, are interested enough to want to. People then know more and can do more.

- **Contentment.** In addition to being a sense of serenity or relief, this is also, Fredrickson says, the secure feeling of being accepted and cared for by others. Contentment allows individuals to appreciate the moment and feel connected with the people and world around them. Contentment also gives people the chance to reflect on a recent experience and integrate the resulting new growth into their personalities and view of the world around them (including their job). It allows for more development, more understanding, and more personal resources to positively take on the next challenge that awaits them.

Being responsible for your employees' happiness isn't about creating a line item in the budget of unlimited miniature golf or a free-flowing chocolate fountain. It's about creating a workplace culture that allows your people to sustain a positive and flexible attitude about themselves, their coworkers, and the work they're doing. When you're able to offer an environment that encourages optimism, challenge, and the time to process the learning that comes from every experience good or bad, you'll have a team that works together well. It will be one that is innovative rather than defensive, driven by the positive meaning behind the work it does, and one that cares about each other's well-being and safety.

17

Great leaders make their people cry

A couple of years ago, the chairman of Rackspace, a fast-growing Web hosting company that's regularly on Fortune's Best Companies to Work For list, asked me to spend 2 weeks interviewing its employees who deeply love their work. The main question: What makes you proud to be a "Racker?"

In one interview, the CEO described a time when he felt especially proud of his people. It was during an emergency years ago when, he said, everything they worked for over the previous 9 years was "on the razor's edge." A truck had crashed into their data center, threatening to destroy the physical plant.

As these things typically happen, it was at night. But it was "all hands on deck" for everyone, and the parking lot was as full at 2 a.m. as it would be at 2 p.m. Inside the building, everyone was there, he said, with his eyes moistening, his throat tightening with emotion. Their children, in PJs, slept on the floor by their parents' cubicles. "I didn't ask them to come," he said. "Word just got out somehow, and everyone was there, on the phones, taking very difficult calls from upset customers, doing what they had to do to keep us up and running."

Another employee emotionally told the story of another near disaster. A Florida customer had to be evacuated in advance of a hurricane. Rackspace techs duplicated their servers, adding them to Rackspace servers already operational in San Antonio. They told their customer to forward all their phone calls to San Antonio so that the Florida company's customers would never know the difference. Then they cleared out a few cubicles in San Antonio so that their Florida customer could relocate some people and keep their business up and running while the wind blew. The wind did blow, destroying the Florida building. But the business prevailed. Because of caring.

Another hurricane, by the name of Katrina, brought thousands of survivors into San Antonio. Graham Weston, the chairman, donated a vacant department store property he owned to be used as a shelter for the incoming. In a matter of just a few hours, Rackers cleaned out the building and set up 2,500 cots, a cafeteria, men's and women's showers, even a beauty parlor. They also set up computer stations and cable televisions (it pays to have at least one techie in the family, doesn't it?) so that the survivors could keep up with the news and reach out to scattered friends and family.

One Racker emotionally told of his *proud* moment: The first person to get off the first bus from New Orleans was an elderly lady who broke into tears. And the human aspect of what he was doing went straight to his heart. Three days later, he finally went home for a little shut-eye.

While interviewing an executive admin, I asked her what's special about working for her boss. It wasn't the money. It wasn't the cool factor of working for the chairman. It wasn't the array of Beemers, Mercedes, and Land Rovers in the parking lot—and the prosperity possibilities that those cars represent. It was her children.

"He always remembers my children," she said through tears of her own. "He never forgets their birthdays and Christmases. Never."

Managers who are "just okay" know how to get people to come to work—largely by disciplining the slackers. Great managers know how to move their people to action. They help their employees make the connections of the human impact of what they do: how their efforts restore hope, relieve pain, and bring beauty into the world.

Great managers know how to move their people to action.

This level of deep caring is enough to move people to more than just action. It's enough to move them to tears.

TRUTH

18

Better questions lead to better answers

One of the joys of taking on a new managerial role is the expectation that finally you'll be able to engage your time in excellent *thinking* about the business. This is your chance to leave the actual heavy lifting of doing the job itself to that star performer in line behind you. And this, to a very large extent, would be true. After all, if you're still doing the work you did, you are being way overpaid—and you haven't opened up that opportunity for professional development for the rest of your team eager to fill the hole you left when you took the promotion. In which case, you're doing your own job wrong.

To do your job right, you must dedicate much of your time equipping your team to live without you. Your role is to teach them how to take on the job you did yesterday. And do it even better than you did. So your people are going to be coming to you with lots of questions. And it will be your responsibility to lead them to even better answers that you fondly embraced when you had the job.

Here's the wrinkle: If you rely on what you knew yesterday to help your team take your place tomorrow, you're already giving them old information. Leadership is not about delivering your best thinking packaged as answers from the past. Business realities are transforming so quickly that the best way to prepare your team to replace you is to teach your people to ask the absolute best questions they can.

> To do your job right, you must dedicate much of your time equipping your team to live without you.

That's change *leadership*, which elevates your role in the company far above change management (which all your competitors are focusing on; too bad for them). This is going to take some nerve on your part.

Jeff Nally, organization developer–executive coaching for Humana, Inc., offers these keys to breakthrough change leadership:

■ **Slow down by asking powerful exploratory questions.** Your team may not yet be practiced in discerning between *really important* pressing issues and *merely interesting* pressing issues. The emotional heat around some urgent concern might not be a true indicator of its long-term value to the company. Help your team pick out the high-value issues that must be resolved for the strategic benefits of your organization's objectives. And teach them to leave the other distracting inconsequentials unattended to, no matter how noisy they might be.

Instead of immediately diving into the presenting problem, ask your people, "How clear is your thinking about this issue right now?" "On a scale of one to ten, how big a priority is this for you right now? What would make it a ten for you?" "Cast yourself into the future, 3 weeks from now. Do you expect this to be as important then as it feels to you now?" "What new ideas have you already had that you would do well to acknowledge before you figure out what other solutions there might be to this immediate problem?"

■ **Make sure that their assumptions are up-to-date, not stuck in yesterday.** What old assumptions, experiences, facts, or feelings are they carrying forward to the current day that no longer exist or might be holding them back in some way? What is the *negative dominant logic* that they can set aside or get rid of entirely so that they can have fresh thinking about the problems before them today?

Is their approach relative to their own changing roles in the organization up to date? Assuming your team members' roles have changed somewhat over time, maybe it's just not their job anymore to be concerned about the presenting issue. Or maybe their skills and newly elevated perspectives have given them new mastery over an issue's extenuating conditions. And now they can attack it from above, rather than from below.

■ **Help all your employees (not just your leaders) refresh their thinking about who they are, what direction their career is going in, and what will fulfill them.** The question "What do you *really* want?" might result in a sardonic laugh and this immediate response: "To hold on to my job." Granted, depending on what's going on in your company and market at the time, that might be the best instant response. But as soon as you can get people to look up from the initial problem, be their coach to improve their own thinking about their crucial decisions about career and life. This could be your most valuable tool for engaging people and retaining your essential talent for the long run.

Don't just manage change. Lead it. And you'll probably find that your own career blossoms as old questions make way for exciting answers to new ones.

TRUTH
19

Individual passion builds a passion-fueled customer service culture

You want your people to be passionate about their work. You definitely want them to be passionate about helping their customers. It would be nice if they were passionate about helping each other. Are you making it easy for your people to keep that passion engine fueled? If they're the slightest bit shy about exuberantly expressing the joy of their work, you've got some work of your own to do.

A few years ago, I had a fantastic experience with a call center rep for a major financial services company. After going through the dreaded automated menu of multiple options, I heard a cheerful voice saying, "May I help you?"

What followed was a one-of-a-kind conversation. No script, just patient listening while I ranted in a somewhat disorganized way. After I slowed down, she gave me essential information that I didn't even know I needed. When I thanked her lavishly for her wonderful service, she rhapsodized about how much she loves taking care of customers' needs. Then suddenly she got shy.

She didn't want anyone to know about what a great job she does. After I asked for her name (which she reluctantly gave me one piece at a time), I then asked, "Who do I talk to about how wonderful you are?" After putting me on hold for half a heartbeat, she came back with an audible sigh of relief to report that they have a "compliment line." "Fantastic," I said. "But it's broken," she said. Which was just fine by her, she said, because she feels really uncomfortable being in the limelight of praise.

So, I did what anyone would do: I took the bull by the horns (probably the only bull available on Wall Street these days) and wrote a letter directly to the company chairman. I've heard nothing in response. Seems that the compliment line might be broken in the C-suite as well.

When employees are reluctant to haul their lights out from under the proverbial bushel, more than just themselves and their careers suffer. The entire company culture suffers, and, by extension, perhaps its bottom line. Here we have an employee who is positively over the moon about her job. (It's not hard to stand out from the crowd in a call center, but how many truly achieve that distinction?) And she does it so well that a fanatical customer writes to the chairman to rave. And still that spark of delight is allowed to peter out. Why not capture that spark, feed it some air, and let it spread throughout your entire culture?

How contagious could that enthusiasm be if she were encouraged to toot her horn—perhaps just a little bit beyond her own limits of what she would consider appropriate? (Sometime in her past, an influential person might have told her that it is unladylike to seek attention and claim credit for a job well done. Or maybe she was taught that being enthusiastic about getting joy from her work was undignified.)

Some people just don't like to brag or rhapsodize. And it's easy for managers to overlook those quiet people glowing in the corner. But a culture-wide emphasis on encouraging people to tell their stories of how they delivered over-the-top service to their customers will encourage these people to speak up. And when the chorus of joy grows and grows, so will the *passion literacy* of your company culture.

When you encourage your people to brag, you're discovering which employees are high-potential talent who deserve to be cultivated. You will find out what specific skills and passions solidify that bond between your company and your customers. And you'll create a positive culture that celebrates high service and high passion.

> When you encourage your people to brag, you're discovering which employees are high-potential talent who deserve to be cultivated.

Start building the passion-literate culture early in your employees' tenure with their team. Ask candidates this question: What dream came true for you when you said yes to your last job offer? The question will surprise them, and will probably make them pause for a few seconds of reflection. But notice who answers most quickly and thoroughly. Those people are in touch with their individual sense of passion. And they'll bring it to work to rejuvenate your team's passion—especially around customer service.

Begin every meeting—preferably a weekly group meeting—with this question: What great thing happened in your job today or this week?

The change might be a little slow to take hold. But once people realize that it is not only safe to be exuberant about their jobs and customer service but also actually expected, you'll have a passion-driven team eager to step up to help your customers, each other, and you.

TRUTH

20

Authentic is better than clever

In 1950, movie actor James Stewart played Elwood P. Dowd, the pixilated best friend of a 6ft… well, 6 ft. 3 (and a half) imaginary (as if you needed to be told that part) white rabbit named Harvey. Dowd's charm is not the companionship of the bunny, though; it's the exceedingly, consistently guileless, open-faced, courteous way he treats people. In the movie's key moment, he says, "My mother told me, 'Elwood, you must be oh so smart. Or oh so pleasant.' Well, for years I was smart. I recommend pleasant."

Every day you are faced with a similar choice in the way you lead your people. How you make that choice reflects your personal values and what you believe is the essential foundation of a healthy, functioning relationship. Only this choice isn't between pleasant and smart; it's between *authentic* and *clever*. And what's cool about this choice is that if you make it right, you won't have to make it at all.

Choose authenticity every time. Authenticity gives you huge returns on your investment of courage and backbone. It gives you clarity in uncertain, confusing times. It helps you be consistent in the way you establish your expectations from your people. And your people know what they can consistently expect from *you*. You are believed and trusted without suspicion of subtext and subterfuge. And when you make a mistake (and you will), you will be forgiven.

Sure, authenticity may seem like the obvious choice, especially while you're sitting there, all comfortable in your chair, reading this book. Authenticity is actually scary. It is the adventurous choice demanding courage, the ability to meet painful decisions head on, the willingness not to be in control all the time, and the faith to trust your people to do the right thing with the truth and reality that you give them unfailingly. Authenticity demands honesty, even when it means that you might not be fair or popular. You stand to lose a lot, at times, by being real with your people. But if your reputation is being more clever than authentic, you stand to lose much more, much more often.

Choose authenticity every time.

It's sometimes difficult, though, to resist the temptation to choose the *clever* way. As a manager, you're being paid to think a couple of steps ahead, and that requires cleverness. But the wrong kind of cleverness can erode the healthy, open environment that authenticity has built. Then maybe you don't communicate as much as you know as often as you can with your employees as you once did. Management fads start looking like fun experiments to see if you can boost your group's productivity a couple of notches, which is especially attractive if you're in a highly competitive environment. Little games, overt and covert, start seeping into your group's culture. People start wondering what you're really up to. And then they start wondering what each other is up to. And they start getting competitive with each other. Then no one's happy. And it stays that way.

> The wrong kind of cleverness can erode the healthy, open environment that authenticity has built.

Here's the fun part: A track record for authentic leadership buys you permission to be clever. Your reputation for straightforward dealings and honest communication will help you bank the trust currency you can then use to think several steps ahead and creatively (and honestly, and legally) work the system to your business's advantage.

Here's how to know when authenticity is essential: You use it to *lead* your people.

Here's how to know when clever is okay: You use it to *serve* your people.

Keep that distinction in mind, and you'll be oh-so trusted. And I recommend trusted.

TRUTH

21

Retention begins with hello

There's a time machine that will take you right back to those wacky, wonderful teenage years. You remember: You were painfully aware of every single thing you did, afraid that one little misstep would reveal to the world the geek that you were afraid you really were. This agonizing self-consciousness was compounded if you were the new kid in school. You didn't know your way around. A secret code divided the cool from the un-. Most people were standoffish. But just as bad: Some people seemed too eager to be your friend. You could fall in with the wrong crowd without realizing it.

And now, ladies and gentlemen, children of all ages, we've got your time machine right here. Step right up and take a look. But don't get too close or you'll get sucked into the vortex known as First Week on a New Job! See how the funny mirrors distort your self-esteem! Marvel at how the floor plans change under your very feet, making you lost and late for every appointment. No! Don't let Overly Friendly Guy touch you! You'll be marked as a Loser forever! Listen to the whispers and the laughter! Hear that? It's you they're talking about. Doomed to eat lunch alone for the rest of your life! Ha! Ha! Ha! Ha!

You've had First Weeks yourself. And, unless you have the self-regard of granite, you know how it feels to be the insecure new hire. But you must have done okay, because now you're the manager. And now newcomers are worried about what you're thinking about *them*. With all the stress and emotions swirling around a new hire's first week on the job, you can be confident that perceptions are skewed and, without your guidance and attention, she may be coming to some strange conclusions about your team, its culture, and who really has the power to get things done.

> Unless there's a death in the family, nothing is more important on your schedule than your new hire's first week.

Your job is to help your new hire get the right start. Otherwise, someone else will step in to fill that need—someone who may not have your team's best interests at heart. If you do it, you'll know that it will get done right:

- **Don't assign a buddy. Be the buddy.** Unless there's a death in the family, nothing is more important on your schedule than your new hire's first week. If you're there for the insignificant questions ("Do we pay for our own coffee or is it free?"), your new employee will feel more comfortable going to you for questions like "Doesn't Joe's request violate the Sarbanes-Oxley Act?" You don't want anyone else to have the chance to answer that.

- **Fill her lunch docket.** If you have a tightly knit team, book the big table at the best restaurant your budget allows and have a welcome-aboard lunch her *very first day* as your team member. Then make sure every lunch hour that first week is booked with individuals from your team, starting with you. If your team isn't so tight, start and end the week with lunch with you, and ask your most positive employees to eat with her during the middle three days.

- **Give her a project to complete that first week.** Give her something meaningful and moderately challenging to do so that she closes out her first 5 days with the satisfaction of accomplishment. Make sure the project makes her circulate throughout the team and even the organization as a whole so that she can meet more people and get a better understanding of how all the pieces work together.

- **Give her a break.** Remember that your employee is under tremendous emotional pressure during the first few days—even months—on the job. She may have landed the job of her dreams that she competed mightily for. But still, with so much at stake, she's going to be self-conscious and nervous. And that could show up in weird ways. She's not herself yet.

- **Don't rush this process.** Your new hire represents the best choice among all the applicants for that position. So, take the time now to welcome her well. Otherwise, you might have to do it again. And that will be with your second choice.

TRUTH

22

The bad will do you good

You might not believe in divine retribution, but you have an employee who makes you wonder what you did in the past—or past life—to deserve this nightmare now. Whatever it was, it must have been pretty bad.

He gets the job done, and then some, so you can't ding him on performance. Darn it. But he has zero respect for authority, not to mention lesser social conventions like, say, socks. His work schedule seems to be synchronized to a time zone on the other side of the planet. So you can just forget about him showing up to any regular meetings, which is just fine by you anyway.

He's subversive, sarcastic, hard to motivate, and impossible to threaten. When your more gentle creative employees come up with a good idea, they politely propose it to the group asking, "… why not?" But when he comes up with an idea, he's in your face, demanding to know, "*Why the hell not?*"

He clearly thinks you're a doofus. And worse yet, he has the power to make you think that maybe he's right. He's a walking poke-in-the-eye, dastardly disguised—but just barely—as a human being. Ah… mavericks. You gotta love them.

No. Really. You *have* to love him. He could be the best thing that has happened to you. Mavericks are passionate, revolutionary, ingenious, independent, completely dependable. (You just have to figure out what they're dependable *for* and then go with that.) They're the ones who take nice little companies and transform them into roaring change-machines that write not only the new code but also the new vocabulary and rules.

He could be the best thing that has happened to you.

Great or beloved companies are started or spun on the ideas of mavericks. Apple, of course. Whole Foods. ING Direct. Patagonia. Pixar. FedEx. Industrial Light and Magic. Cirque du Soleil. Wikipedia. Craig's List. If you have a maverick in your group, whisper a silent prayer of thanks, and then hang on tight.

Your main job is to keep mavericks on your team—and to keep your team from wringing their necks when you're not looking:

- **Give them a goat.** In horseracing, high-strung horses used to be assigned pet goats to keep them placid in their stalls (hence the saboteur's expression *to get one's goat*). Everyone needs a friend, even mavericks. And mavericks especially could use a trusted counterpart to bounce ideas off of and to share insecurities and questions with. If you notice your maverick congenially pairing off with another coworker, find ways to keep them together. Don't try to engineer the relationship according to preconceived ideas of what a good goat is. You're not necessarily looking for someone who's meek to complement the one who's wild. Even if you're looking at two mavericks who have found each other, great! Put them together. At least they'll stop bugging everyone else. Maybe.

- **Give them all the latitude they want, without special treatment.** If your company offers some sort of flextime, give your mavericks all the elasticity they'll run with. Just make sure they know you expect to actually see some productivity. If they do their best work at 1 a.m., there's comfort in knowing that at least you're getting good training for running a global team.

- **Hear them out.** Much of that in-your-face energy that they bring to meetings (or conversely, the what's-the-point-of-even-trying energy) comes from a past of being discounted by people who dismissed their originality. Be the first manager who actually listens, even to the point of asking them questions that draw out additional ideas about implementation, distribution, marketing, and so on. Be the one they know they can trust with a half-baked, but brilliant, notion. And they'll see you as one of *their* team members who might not be such a doofus after all.

> Be the one they know they can trust with a half-baked, but brilliant, notion.

- **Ask them if they have any friends.** Believe it or not, they just might. And you can bet these people are just as smart and visionary as your staff mavericks. If you mix more brilliance in your group, you could end up with a well-balanced team of collaboration, breakthrough ideas, and the round-the-clock energy to make those ideas reality.

Who knows? Maybe those mavericks will make you their mascot.

23

Your biggest complainer may be your best supporter

Who doesn't love that *Jerry Maguire* moment when Jerry, fed up with being forced to perform in a way that's counter to his values, writes and releases to the world a scathing "manifesto?" The next morning, he arrives at work to a standing ovation from all his coworkers. And, inevitably, he receives the invitation from management to seek his fortune elsewhere.

If some sort of machine could capture all the thoughts of anyone who has ever watched this movie, there would be transoceanic freighters full of little thought balloons that read, "Yup, that's me. I'm Jerry." But when you're in management, you may be Jerry in your heart, but you're the boss in fact. And this is no longer the Jerry-era of internal e-mails. This is the age of the blog, Facebook, and Twitter. Welcome.

There's the guy I know who actually did pull a Jerry, unburdening himself on a publicly accessible company blog. And, as the young legend has it, he actually came to work the next day to coworkers applauding from their cubicles. Unlike the movie Jerry, though, this guy kept his job. I know this because the CEO told me himself. As a point of pride.

The fact that this Jerry still has his job speaks volumes about the company. The founders and the leaders can take it on the chin—and still be glad to see this guy in the morning. Jerry is irreplaceable, a valuable employee who has been with the company from its earliest days. And although maybe the blog might not have been the best space for airing his grievances, what was done was, well, done. Out there in the universe forever.

What Jerry really did was put the company's culture to the test. The leaders have long said that they want a passion-fueled company where all employees are free to speak their mind. But, when employees get passionate, it's not always a happy passion. And what might be perceived as *negative passion* can be really embarrassing. But it's also extremely informative.

In this particular case, Jerry, who had been with the company from almost Day One, was worried that the company culture that everyone had so carefully cultivated and cherished was being diluted by waves of newly hired middle managers who (mistakenly) assumed that their power lay in blocking freely flowing information from the rank and file and their beloved CEO. Passionate rank and file can tell you so much about what's really going on in your company's culture: how healthy your network of trust is among all your employees, that essential innovation is being undermined by turf battles, or that a team lead on the graveyard shift is jeopardizing your entire Asia operation because he prefers volume over quality when it comes to customer service-resolution reports. These are the kinds of things you won't know unless your people care enough, are angry enough, and feel safe enough to tell you. Over and over again—or publicly—if that's what it takes to get your attention.

As your team's leader, you can't prevent your employees from venting their frustrations on a public blog. Your power lies in helping your employees trust that they don't have to go to such extremes to get the results they're looking for. To achieve this shift, you have to make your office a safe place where people with issues can come and let 'er rip:

> These are the kinds of things you won't know unless your people care enough, are angry enough, and feel safe enough to tell you.

- ■ **Learn to love complaints.** If you yearn for the command-control days when managers had the last word, you were born several decades too late. In most workplaces that embrace employee engagement and foster innovativeness, all employees are encouraged to "own" their roles in the organization. It's only fair, because, unlike any other time in modern workplace history, they're directly responsible for their own outcomes. When an employee is so worked up about something going on in the company that he is willing to put his job on the line, that's a sign of caring more about the business than his own best self-interests. Annoying as that might be for you, that's actually a good thing.
- ■ **Learn to welcome the complainer.** Some people are real pains in the posterior—precisely because they're passionate about the prospect of your enterprise. The ones who don't really give a darn… well, they're awfully quiet. It's quite possible that

they're passively disengaged. Which is okay if you don't mind giving valuable salaries to human doorstops. But being passively disengaged is just one step away from being disengaged. And that's where you'll begin to have real problems with toxic whiners infecting the entire workplace with their bummer attitude. Weirdly, the inflamed blogger who spews his fury publicly might actually be the better employee.

■ **Let the complainer have his say.** People go public with their rage when they're confident that they won't be heard privately. He knows what's really going on in your company. He's got valuable information and insights for you that you might not get anywhere else. And he cares so much about your business that he's willing to put his job on the line. Let him take that risk behind closed doors. Don't make him have to resort to HTML.

Public embarrassment of the blog kind is really too bad—maybe even horrifying, depending on the content and the timing. But don't be afraid of the truth. Even when it's the hard truth. The real truth is that if it gets to the point where your people have to go public, you probably have only yourself to blame.

TRUTH

24

You can sell an unpopular decision

The trouble with making a really difficult choice is that someone is always going to hate it. And some of the decisions you make—especially the difficult ones—are going to negatively impact at least one employee. In fact, the more difficult the decision was for you, the worse it's going to be for the employees who had a stake in the losing proposition. The "losers" may feel that their ideas were discredited or, worse, dismissed. And maybe the losers might also feel that their job is at risk, if not, indeed, already obliterated. If the decision you had to make results in a significant layoff, no one's going to be happy with you—except for perhaps senior management.

No mentally healthy adult expects to be happy with every twist and happenstance that comes along in life and work. But a hard knock is still a hard knock. And no amount of mental health is going to change that. Researchers are discovering, though, that one detail will make even the bitterest horse pill of bad news go down more smoothly: that's the employees' confidence that they were treated fairly in the decision-making process.

If the advice to be fair in your decision making seems laughably obvious, that's good. But that's not the point. First of all, sometimes you can't be fair in the decision you finally come to. But the way you arrive at a decision can always be fair. And then (here's the not-so-obvious point), the extraordinary efforts you take to make sure all employees know that the decision-making process itself was fair will take you a long way to selling your decision and achieving employee buy-in (even from those on the "losing" end).

> The way you arrive at a decision can always be fair.

Studies have also shown that employees' confidence in process fairness actually reduces the likelihood of retaliation and resistance. One study that tracked 1,000 terminated employees shows that only 1 percent of the employees who felt that they were at least treated fairly filed wrongful termination suits. But 17 percent of those who felt they were treated unfairly filed lawsuits. Researchers have also linked faith in fairness to lower incidents of employee theft and voluntary resignations.

But fairness is in the eye of the employee. You may have your own ideas about what fair means, but when it comes to selling a difficult decision, the only definition that counts is the one your employees' hold. Generally, this means the following:

Fairness is in the eye of the employee.

- They feel that they had the chance to have some level of input into the decision-making process. If the final decision affects them, it would only seem, well, fair, to give them a chance to voice their opinion and perhaps provide a determining idea or insight.

- They have confidence that the decision was made in a way that's consistent with the practices and culture of the organization. The decision must have been made based on accurate information. There was little or no favoritism. And managers can transparently trace the various key decision points for employees to follow and understand.

- The news is announced respectfully by an appropriately senior manager. Rule of thumb: The worse the news affecting the larger number of people, the more senior the executive must be. You must explain the process as fully as you can and then answer the employees' questions—and listen to the barrage of objections. And there will be many, to be sure. But employees who are unhappy with your decision aren't necessarily likely to quit over it, especially if they have the chance to express their opinions.

Rumor has it that the employment contract is over. But that's not entirely true; it has just changed. Instead of the paternalistic promise of guaranteed salary for life, it is now more of an agreement struck between adults. Your employees are now truly stakeholders. And, as such, they expect explanations of the decisions you make for the business—especially the ones that negatively affect their livelihoods.

If your decision can withstand the light of scrutiny, you can sell it to your employees. But you have to treat them with the dignity and respect they deserve as adults and show them the process by which you made that decision. After all, it's only fair.

TRUTH
25

Flex is best

Workplace flexibility isn't a matter of more private time for employees as much as it is a matter of more control of *all* their time. And employers benefit as a result. Studies of workplace flexibility report higher engagement, more employee commitment, greater retention, and improved performance (even greater on-time performance in some manufacturing or distribution centers) when employees have more control over the way they mix their work and private time .

Over recent years, companies have increasingly set policies allowing some kind of workplace flexibility. Flexibility could take any number of forms: staggered hours, telecommuting, split or shared shifts, and even distance working, where an employee works out of her home, her briefcase, a frequent fliers' lounge, or a cubicle at the FedEx Office. But it's one thing for companies to offer flexible work plans. It's an entirely different matter for managers to actually allow it. Even though the pro-flexibility policy might have been

Studies of workplace flexibility report higher engagement, more employee commitment, greater retention, and improved performance.

hatched in the cool, crisp air of the C-suite, executives wisely leave its actual implementation to the managers who are best positioned to decide whether it's a realistic way to run their individual teams on a day-to-day basis.

But many managers, focusing on the short-term issues of work in the trenches, are still seeing that the upfront hassle of setting up a program in their teams isn't worth the long-term benefits. Managers looking at flexible work arrangements can immediately imagine problems with perceived favoritism (even discrimination), lack of control over how employees use their time to maximize productivity, and communication issues. It's understandable that many managers resist the risk that flexible workplaces pose.

Don't mistake your prerogative to say yes as a blanket permission to say no. It could be easier than you think to implement a flexible workplace:

■ **Double-check with HR in HQ.** Make sure that there's commitment to flexibility at the very top. See what policies are already in place on the corporate level. There might be an incentive program that encourages managers to experiment with flexible arrangements. Or the organizational effectiveness office might send a team to help you with the planning and considerations you'll face.

Don't mistake your prerogative to say yes as a blanket permission to say no.

■ **Recruit your employees as your collaborators.** Work with them as a group to decide what kinds of flexible arrangements would work best for them. Give them a sense of ownership in the planning of the initial stages, and they'll take on some responsibility toward its success.

■ **Let them know what *your* concerns are.** As their co-adventurer on this experiment, you have specific needs that your employees should help you with. You might have trust or control concerns. So, let your team know that you'll need their help in reassuring you, especially during this early phase.

■ **Expect mistakes, disappointments, and process reviews.** Just know in advance that there will be some missteps. Some employees won't be able to resist the temptation of taking advantage of the program. *You* might not be able to resist the urge to shorten the control leash on your employees, especially if you're subconsciously worried that you're losing control that you value.

■ **Get support from your colleagues.** You don't have to pioneer this by yourself. Seek out the managers of other departments and business units that are implementing flexible work schedules. Find out what is working for them and what mistakes you can avoid making. If it doesn't already exist, create a community of managers sharing their best practices with each other and then extending that learning to other divisions in your company.

■ **Get some of that good stuff for yourself.** It may dawn on you one morning while you're stuck in traffic that there's no reason why you can't enjoy a flexible work schedule, too. Your people know how to find you. The work is getting done. You've demonstrated to your boss that the flexible work schedule is actually enhancing retention. Why not? You've got a great case to bring to your boss, who will then have a great case to bring to leaders all the way up the organization.

TRUTH

26

Nobody cares if you don't mean to be mean

Everyone has a story about at least one mean boss. Oddly, though, there isn't a commensurate number of people who have stories about being bully bosses themselves. You know the type. You see them on the evening news magazine shows: the folks who brandish guns at work; who discriminate against a race, gender, or religion in their promotion practices and then brag about it; bosses who hang their employees "in effigy" for the rest of the department to ridicule. The brutality of that kind of behavior is just so plain to see— unmistakable and inarguable.

But the most common behaviors that beat down the human spirit aren't so easy to catch and stop the first time. What is truly unacceptable? The first time the boss pitches a screaming fit? Or the thirtieth time? The insults flung in private behind closed doors? Or the public humiliation in the store full of customers? In the comfort and safety of emotional distance, it might be natural to think, "Well, that's easy. No screaming fit is acceptable. I would never tolerate a barrage of personal insults, regardless of where it happened. I'd quit the first time it happened." But when there's rent to be paid and a family to feed, the first screaming fit is tolerated, as is the thirtieth, as is the one hundred thirtieth. And the insults in front of the customers? Oh! That was awful, but it's over now. And the boss hasn't mentioned it since. There wasn't even an apology, so maybe there wasn't anything to apologize for. You were just being sensitive.

Do you think you have become a mean boss without realizing it?

But you're the boss now. Do you think you might have become a mean boss somewhere along the line without realizing it? If you've been exposed to abusive treatment in your life, whether it was from an overly harsh parent or from an early supervisor who vented frustrations out on the youngest member of the company (you), you might have become desensitized to cruel behavior.

You're really a nice person at heart. And it astounds you to think that people have become frightened of you. How could you have lost your sense of the difference between being a boss who gets things done by leading his people and a boss who gets things done by beating his people? Maybe it's not about what you think about yourself, but what you actually do. The Workplace Bullying Institute put together a list of 25 most common behaviors in its 2003 Report on Abusive Workplaces. Here are just a few examples, in no particular order of importance or prevalence:

- Falsely accused someone of errors not actually made
- Stared, glared, was nonverbally intimidating, and clearly showing hostility
- Discounted a person's thoughts or feelings in meetings
- Exhibited presumably uncontrollable mood swings in front of the group
- Stole credit for work done by others
- Used confidential information about a person to humiliate privately or publicly
- Assigned undesirable work as punishment
- Made undoable demand—workload, deadlines, duties—for a target employee
- Encouraged the person to quit or transfer rather than to face more mistreatment
- Yelled, screamed, threw tantrums in front of others to humiliate a person
- Made up rules on-the-fly

After looking at this list, can you honestly say that you lead your employees by elevating their self-esteem and what great things they're capable of? Or do you drive them by leveraging their fear and shame?

You may be unpleasantly surprised to see more of yourself in this list than you'd like. And you may be shocked to see how far you've gone down the wrong road. Very few people begin their careers with the ambition of becoming a mean boss. But no one aspires to work for one. And no one deserves to, either.

> Can you honestly say that you lead your employees by elevating their self-esteem?

You may not mean to be mean. And you can intentionally make the necessary behavior changes that will transform you into an inspiring leader who cares for the team's well-being. And your people, in return, will support and encourage your efforts.

TRUTH

27

Controlling your temper is a labor-saving device

What's your hot button? What puts you at risk of losing it? Losing sight of the cost/benefit ratio of acting out on your anger? Dealing with petty, immature skirmishes between employees who snookered you into thinking they were adults?

When people stand in your doorway with "Can we talk?" written on their face, rarely are they bearing a basket of kitten kisses and posies for you. When it's a petty interpersonal hiccup, you'll hear about it. If there is a stupid person doing indifferent, sloppy, and thoughtless work, you'll hear about it. If someone has discovered that there is a lot of currency to be had for being perpetually and righteously outraged, you hear about it. And *you'll* be expected to do something about it.

How many times in your career so far have you been tempted to holler, "What are we, *in Kindergarten*" This is where you might lose your cool.

It's tempting to assume here that if you have achieved managerial status you've probably already dealt with whatever hair-trigger emotions you might have. But you and I both have seen too many instances of managers with a low boiling point not to think that a little introspection now and then might be a good idea.

> When people stand in your doorway with "Can we talk?" written on their face, rarely are they bearing a basket of kitten kisses and posies for you.

Losing your cool puts you at risk of losing more than just your temper. It strains trust between you and your employees. You totally lose your dignity (which is significant when you're trying to manage on a platform of level-headed leadership). It wounds tender feelings, sometimes irreparably (and maybe even feloniously). It can shatter trust. And it gives your employees something to laugh at you about. Behind your back.

So, no matter where you are in your professional journey, maybe it's time to quickly review and tweak how you react to triggering situations. Or pass this truth on to someone who might benefit from it—and then duck:

- **Be your own fly on the wall.** Researchers at Ohio State University and the University of Michigan call it *self-distancing*. In a study, they found that putting yourself in a mindset in which you're viewing the situation at an imaginary distance helps protect yourself from getting caught up in a web of escalating fury. Taking a mental step back can help you temper your rage.

- **Give yourself time to react.** *Their* emergency doesn't have to be *your* emergency, unless you allow it. Unless the situation has something to do with a building on fire, you can likely wait 24 to 48 hours before making a considered pronouncement on the matter being shoved into your face.

- **Know the difference between the facts and your interpretation of what's behind the behavior.** Managers need to be insightful about human behavior and motivation. That doesn't mean you have to be a mind-reader. It just means to follow the advice of that bumper sticker spotted on many a hippie van: Don't believe everything you think.

- **Make someone else's problem... someone else's problem.** You can provide an ear, but you don't always have to provide a solution.

- **Know what your boundaries are and expect everyone to respect them—including yourself.** When you're confident that you have the power to honor yourself and your own needs in the little ways that the people in your workday try to chisel away at your boundaries, you know that you can afford to stay powerfully calm when facing down the big-stakes issues. Then those little straws won't pile up, which means that there will be no *last straw* to ignite your own personal kaboom.

- **Don't lose sight of what you really want in the long run.** If your immediate emotional reaction has even the slightest tinge of self-righteousness to it, dollars to donuts that acting out on that reaction will move you further away from your objectives. While you're giving yourself time to react (see the second bulleted point in this list), review exactly what your end game is and whether your emotions are supporting that end game.

So, in answer to your question, yes, we are in kindergarten. In management, sometimes you're the kindergartener, sometimes you're the teacher. It won't always be your job to make every booboo all better. But it is always your job not to make it any worse.

28

There is no "but" in "I'm sorry"

If you don't have a reason to apologize to your team every year or so, you're not trying hard enough. Your company is changing under your feet. Your direct reports are learning new skills and abilities. So it's safe to assume that you're also growing in your role. And you're only human. Put those two elements together and you've got yourself the perfect setting for screwing up now and then. Expecting yourself to perform perfectly—with absolutely no leeway for a blunder now and again—creates the perfect setting for screwing up royally.

Being a great manager isn't about being perfect. It's about being flawed for all the right reasons. Think of it as good debt versus bad debt. Ideally, no one wants to be in debt at all. But considering the realities of modern life, we're going to be in debt. And the best discipline is to be in debt in ways that will benefit us in the long run. A little ding now lays the foundation for massive growth within the foreseeable future.

> Being a great manager isn't about being perfect. It's about being flawed for all the right reasons.

Likewise, given the realities of working in a rapidly changing business environment, you're going to owe a debt of apology to the people who work for you. So the mistakes you make as a manager should be the kind of mistakes that help you grow as a person or professional. You want them to be the kind of mistakes that will help your entire team grow by learning from your experience. At the very least, they can learn how to apologize in a way that strengthens their team, not undermines it:

- **Gain the perspective you need to understand the extent of the damage.** When you discover that you've blundered, take some time to fully understand its immediate impact and the ripple effects of what you've done. Do this quickly, because all this time your team may be seething. But do it thoroughly. Fully understand the impacts up the organization, and, just as important, down the organization throughout your team. This understanding will help you determine exactly whom you should apologize to and what to say that's relevant to your team.

■ **Make it a *teachable moment* for you, but don't call it a teachable moment when discussing the error with your team.** Honest mistakes—especially those made with the best of intentions—are almost always forgivable by your team (unless you've somehow been saddled with a toxic team of Machiavellian creeps). But superior, self-righteous, sanctimoniousness behaviors hardly ever are. When you're facing down a group of people who are truly and rightfully mad at you or wounded by something you've done, no one wants to hear you say, "So, people, what can we all learn from this?" All they want to hear is "I'm sorry."

■ **Put a period after "I'm sorry," even if it means you have to choke on the urge to follow up with an excuse or mitigating factor.** "I'm sorry, but…" isn't an apology. It's weaseling out. It's also a waste of your breath and valuable company time because you're going to have to apologize all over again, to set things truly right.

■ **Apologize publicly when warranted, but that doesn't let you off the hook for apologizing privately to an individual you've inadvertently wronged.** Managerial mistakes usually have at least two dimensions: the impact on the team and the business, and the more pointed impact on individuals who have been most directly damaged. The public apology may be humiliating. But the private apology shouldn't be frightening. (If you really believe that your physical safety is at risk, put this book down and contact HR for guidance.)

■ **Don't use private apology to recruit a mole.** In your one-on-one apologies, make it about the apology and restoring a healthy, productive relationship with the aggrieved. Resist the temptation to leverage that time to build a secret conduit into learning what the rest of the team is thinking.

■ **Let 'em talk.** Just because you've apologized, that doesn't mean that everything will be magically peachy with your team from that point forward. No matter the size of your error, they're going to need time to get it out of their system. Use that time to actively restore your relationship with them, and eventually the positive will take the place of any remaining rancor.

Remember: When direct reports apologize to their managers, the subtext is "please don't fire me." When managers apologize to their direct reports, the subtext is "please continue to respect me." In both scenarios, the true value of the apology is working together to return to the equilibrium of collaboration, preferably with some new strength and trust where the broken place used to be.

TRUTH

29

Engagement happens one person at a time

Abe is a corporate security expert who has devoted his life to his profession. Born in India to a Muslim family, he moved to the United States as a young man, went to school, discovered corporate security, and started a thriving security consulting firm using his birth name, which was immediately identifiable as being Muslim. Then 9/11 happened, and his practice predictably plummeted. A Secret Service agent friend of his took him aside one day and gave him this advice: "You have a choice. Keep your profession or keep your name. At this point in time, you can't have both. Maybe later, but not right now." Abe chose to keep his profession.

Because he had already converted to Christianity, he felt no religious allegiance to his name. So he adopted his American wife's Anglo-Saxon maiden name. But what about "Abe?" Why did he choose that name? His answer: "Abraham is the last prophet that Christians, Muslims, and Jews together revere. By calling myself Abe, I'm using my name as the symbol of my life's purpose, which is to unify people according to values we all share."

To look at Abe passing in the hallway, this is what you might see: a smiling, friendly guy, dressed in a suit or business casual, with his laminated employee ID hung from a lanyard and tucked into his breast pocket. He's just like any other guy you'd pass in the hallway. There's probably nothing especially deep on his mind, you might assume. He's just like your other good employees. They show up to work on time. They get the job done reasonably reliably. They come up with good ideas now and then. And they follow the rules. What more do you really need to know about your employees?

But, just like Abe, many of those other employees you'd pass in the hallway have amazing stories to tell about how their work helps them realize their own heroic missions in life.

Their jobs play an essential role in their saga of personal purpose.

Everyone has a story—a saga, actually—of learning, working hard, pursuing his dreams, finding his life's purpose, making tremendous sacrifices, beating the odds, saving his family, saving his children, saving his marriage, saving himself. And, for many of these people, their jobs play an essential role in their saga of personal purpose. Capture some of that passion, and you can use it to fuel your company's mission-critical objectives.

Give your employees the chance to express the fullness of their life's saga and talk about how their jobs intersect with their life's mission. You'll be amazed at the variety of their points of connectivity. You have employees just like Abe who have amazing stories to tell about how their jobs are helping them make dreams come true. Every single one of them has some compelling aspect to his sense of self that's driving him forward. Find out what that certain something is, discover how it links with your company's objectives, and you've got engagement that will outlast any paycheck, any promotion, or any awards ceremony.

You actually have to talk to your employees one person at a time to find out what their story is. This is the *voice of the employee*, but too often it gets aggregated into one huge clump of quantifiable opinions that emerge from surveys. Surveys may be important, but they don't breathe life into the flame of career passion. There are hundreds of books on "do what you love," but when was the last time you saw a book called *The Survey-Driven Life* or *Fill Out Those Surveys, and the Money Will Follow*?

> If you want to truly engage your employees, engage them on the level of their passion.

If you want to truly engage your employees, engage them on the level of *their* passion. If you want to truly engage your employees on the level of their passion, give them the chance to speak from their own hearts, tell their own stories, and inspire each other in the vision that your company is the place that will help them manifest their greatest destinies. One employee at a time.

TRUTH

30

If you're a manager, you're a career coach

No one is in a dead-end job, not even those people who think they are. There is always a way out—even a way up—from any job. Help your employees find that line of sight between what they're doing now and what they'd like to be doing in their future. You are helping develop the future of your entire business.

Managers who help their employees control the quality of their career prospects control the quality of their own prospects, including the high costs of turnover and replacement. Sooner or later, your employees will start looking for their next opportunity. You should have already helped them spot it, plan for it, and train for it (within *your* company, not down the street).

Career pathing—the practice of helping employees identify where they want their careers to go and what steps they need to take to get there—is a people service any company can provide its employees, no matter who they are or where they sit on the org chart.

> Sooner or later, your employees will start looking for their next opportunity.

Before you can advise others, understand how your company maps and tracks the success steps of all its employees throughout the organization. Talk to as many long-tenured, high-performing employees as you can to discover what behaviors, work habits, and transferable skills help them move the most freely throughout the entire organization. What characteristics, knowledge, and initiatives does your company reward beyond the strictly defined skill set of any one particular job?

Then research more job-specific promotion opportunities that might be available to your people. This project actually has two channels: researching the jobs most commonly filled by people in your department looking for any next step, and those jobs most commonly *desired* by your people looking for the next step of their dreams. Discover what skills, education, experiences, and attributes each of these jobs requires. And if a collection of these descriptions doesn't already exist, put one together! A binder with sheet protectors—one page per job description—could do the job just as effectively as an elaborate internal Web site. Just make sure it's always available to your employees to browse through in relative privacy.

And make sure *you're* available to talk to your employees about what might be their next developmental goal.

Make career counseling one of your most important roles in your department. And assume nothing when you speak to your people about their individual ambitions. Let them tell *you* what their ideal next step is. It might not be a promotion for the sake of more money. It might not be a transfer out of your department. It might not even be a job that already exists, but one that you can custom-design for your employee at no additional expense.

In a Tucson call center, a young war veteran was happy in his job as a customer service rep, but he wanted to use the leadership skills he had learned in the Army to help his coworkers develop their own prospects. No specific job title already existed that would officially tap into that employee's drive, so his supervisor helped him design his own job description, folding coaching into his role. In addition to a set number of hours during which he was still expected to take care of customers, he now had permission to use another portion of his workweek to counsel his coworkers on their own performance and prospects.

> Let them tell *you* what their ideal next step is.

And now, instead of being frustrated that his boss didn't see and make good use of his energy (and consequently leaving), this one customer service rep remained on the job. He is still enthused about his work, exciting others about their duties and speaking to community groups of small businesses (his customer base) and high school and college students about what a great company his employer is.

Not only did his supervisor creatively work with him to find a way to stay and grow, he's now helping other prospective employees conclude that they can find their future with this company as well.

TRUTH

31

The candidates you're
seeking may not be
the ones you need

As this book is being written, the United States is suffering record high unemployment rates. One report states that there are 3.5 Americans competing for every job opening. From the perspective of the recruiter, that could be good news: a buyer's market for staffing. Theoretically, you could be having your pick of great talent—if those available candidates were actually qualified for the open positions. On the contrary, though, perhaps it feels like you're still going begging for the best. From what you can tell while sorting resumés and conducting interviews, "All the good ones are taken." Is it really that impossible to catch the eye of great candidates?

Maybe part of your problem is that you're putting out the wrong bait? Have you updated your own expectations for the people who will fit into your team culture? Have your long-term employees matured and moved on to different life priorities without you noticing? Considering how your company has changed over time, might you need to update position responsibilities descriptions? After all, would the best candidate for the position you created and wrote the description for a decade ago be a good fit for that same position today?

Maybe part of your problem is that you're putting out the wrong bait?

Depending on your industry and your geographic location, you probably spent the past 10 years or so positioning your company as a *fun place to work*. Maybe your company isn't so much fun these days, but it's still nice to have that reputation that yours is a company where time flies. In fact, maybe that feeling is still in your online Careers tab.

One company I worked with was so committed to being a tantalizing magnet for high-talent, high-tech resumés that its Careers tab actually featured a candid picture of a poker game in progress, with one guy looking up at the camera while making an *L* on his forehead. Now that's a really fun place to work! Fun, that is, for people who don't want to work, who enjoy burning up the business hours playing poker with others who will gladly tell the world that they're losers.

That message to the outside world during the high-tech company's ramp-up phase might have been fine in its early days. But that was then. And this is, well, now. The early employees grew up. Got married—even the L-guy found someone who would marry him. Had kids. Began to take their work very seriously, especially as the company was positioning itself to go public. They weren't so much interested in the much ballyhooed margarita machines or the fact they could wear flip-flops to work. And they came to resent the sound of pock-pock-pock from the Ping-Pong table down the hall as the new hires took part in the "fun" of the work culture but not so much the "work" part of the work culture.

This company's top talent really didn't want to work with new hires who were attracted to the company because word on the street was that the company was a party place. They wanted to work with serious-minded colleagues who were focused on getting the job done.

If you're getting a rash of losers lining up for the few jobs you have open, it's definitely not because the pickings are slim out there. It could be because your recruitment message is so 2003. Plenty of really wonderful, dedicated, seasoned professionals out there are looking for an opportunity where they can do more than pull down a paycheck or the tap handle for free beer.

If you're in the enviable position of being able to hire new talent for your team, take a proactive role in making sure that you attract the right resumés:

- **Confer with your team already in place.** Beyond what skills and experiences they need from the new hire to help them meet corporate objectives, what kind of person are they looking for as a colleague? To be clear, you're not taking an order from them. The conversation will help everyone gain clarity about what personality and work style would be a good fit in a culture that has evolved while you were focusing on other priorities.

- **Take a tour of your own department.** To an outsider looking at your workspace for the first time, would the posters, decorations, and toys accurately reflect your team culture? Do they overwhelm any emphasis that your employees place on the quality of customer service and high performance? Or do they augment your team's core philosophy that great work and *joie de vivre* go hand in hand?

Are you attracting the right candidates for the right reason? Now's your chance to improve the quality of your bait to improve the quality of your candidates. You're not only helping your company. You're also helping qualified candidates out there who are looking for a great next career move. And you'll be doing your current employees a really big favor.

TRUTH

32

Ask for cheese—you might get the moon

In 1933, John Jay Whitney was strolling through his 600-acre Long Island estate one day when an amusing notion crossed his mind. So he turned to his groundskeeper and said, "Wouldn't it be great to be able to play polo right here?" Then he went on vacation.

When he returned, he came back to discover a lovely, leveled polo field where the gentle, natural swells of Long Island seacoast landscape used to be.

Oops.

Most of us don't think, operate, or make mistakes on the scale of a John Jay Whitney (one of the country's wealthiest men in those times, who started the first venture capital firm, financed Minute Maid orange juice, and *Gone with the Wind* and served as ambassador to Great Britain during the Eisenhower administration). But managers have more power than they know. And they sometimes think aloud. The result? A polo field!

It's hard to imagine that in these days of more democratic, team-based workplace cultures, such a thing can happen. Four words immediately come to mind, though: five-figure shower curtains.

This is not a chapter about executive excesses, by the way. It's about that small reptilian noodle that basks inside all our brains with one assignment only: Do whatever you have to do to keep alive. These days that translates into the mandate of keeping a steady paycheck coming. And for your employees (no matter how egalitarian you pride yourself in being), that translates into two words: "Yes, boss."

> ## Abject hop-to-it-iveness is nothing to be proud of.

Even though we don't like to think of ourselves as whip-cracking leaders, we do like to think of ourselves as the kind of people who know how to get things done—especially via the impassioned dedication and innovative talents of our *team*. But abject hop-to-it-iveness is nothing to be proud of. It's the feudal squeaking of the gecko inside us all that pleads, "Keep feeding me!"

If you have the power to hire and fire, you hold many little reptilian brains in the palm of your hand. Your employees are acutely aware that their advancement and survival may be, for the moment at least, at the service of your pleasure and fancies. If you think you may be getting more than you actually ask for, it's time to do a proportion check:

- **Do you think aloud to the wrong people?** Yes, you should neutralize your inner yes-man by exploring exciting ideas outside the safe, and ever-so-reassuring, confines of your own skull. But if you're sharing all your thoughts with just your direct reports, you may be exchanging your internal cheerleader for a whole cadre of people who are, in fact, paid to tell you you're brilliant.

    If you want real, brutally honest feedback on your latest ideas, build a team of friends and authorities who aren't counting on your goodwill for their rent money. Once you've tested it with trusted and respected people who are meeting their basic needs elsewhere, you can safely bring it to your team and request their feedback, ideas, processes, budgets, and schedules.

- **Are you making it safe for your direct reports to double-check your meaning and intent?** This is an economic era when we build our competitive advantage by bringing things to the world it has never seen before. Few people get ahead in their careers these days by saying, "It can't be done." And that economic climate stifles the "no's" in your department, which could ultimately prove to be very expensive and regrettable for you. So, while you certainly don't want a team made up solely of entrenched "no men," it's good for your entire department to know that it can ask, "Are you sure?"

    > Few people get ahead in their careers these days by saying, "It can't be done."

    If you get that second question, stifle your own inner reptile, and ask a few questions back: What are you seeing that I'm overlooking? Do you see a better (cheaper, more efficient) solution to this problem? Can we get the results we're looking for without such drastic measures? So you think a party on Malta might not be the best way to invest stockholder funds?

    Welcome that double-checking function as a trusted measure against huge mistakes that can change the landscape of your entire business. Give your team permission to say, "Maybe there's a better way." Your successes may be less dramatic, maybe. But your blunders won't be the stuff of cautionary tales 75 years later.

TRUTH

33

You lead better when you get off your pedestal

Depending on when you started your career, you might be more familiar with the old ideas of what managing people is all about: Top down. Command/control. Do as I say, not as I do. Yours is not to question why, yours is to do your job or lose it.

That kind of hierarchical control approach to drawing great work from employees might have worked in the past, but it belongs in the past. You may still find employees willing to slog under such a heavy hand of management, but the really great talent knows better. To keep them on your team, it's time to evolve your own management style.

"Any behaviors that looks like they're hierarchically driven, where you as the manager behave as a broker of information and power, those behaviors should simply be gone," says Craig Ramsay, managing director of the San Francisco Bay office of Sirota Survey Intelligence.

"Managing today means involving and including employees where you might not have ordinarily done it in previous years. It means sharing your responsibilities with them and challenging them to step up and take more on both individually and as a team."

As you consider what behaviors you want to brand your leadership style, you must ask yourself how willing you are to share your managerial power with your entire team.

As you consider what behaviors you want to brand your leadership style, you must ask yourself how willing you are to share your managerial power with your entire team. After you honestly answer that (and assuming that you do want to share power), you'll want to do the following:

- **Treat people the way you want to be treated.** You may be a manager, but you're probably also managed by someone higher up the org chart. Exactly how do you want to be treated by your superiors? In what precise ways do you expect the operating values of your company to play out in your executive group's behaviors? How does it feel to you personally when they fall short of those expectations? Identify what those behaviors are and model them yourself. Don't wait for an official decree to come down from the C-suite.

- **Create your own team employee value proposition.**
Many companies that are seriously invested in cultivating an engagement culture take the time to create what's known as an *employee value proposition*. This is a set of promises to employees about how they can expect to be treated on the job. If your company doesn't have one, create a team value proposition— as a team project. As a group, decide exactly what your team members can promise each other in terms of kindness and respect, truth, free sharing of knowledge, and so on.

- **Be willing to show your own vulnerability.** You're experiencing some fears and concerns of your own about the direction of the business, your marketplace, even about yourself. Your team expects you to share what's on your mind. Showing your vulnerability creates a more humanizing environment that allows your employees to share their own concerns—and even ask each other for help.

- **Know your people as individuals.** It's not your leadership style that should dictate how you behave with your employees. It's how you fulfill their needs from you as their team leader that will make the difference in your effectiveness. Each employee has a different need and expectation. And each one has a different comfort zone in terms of how he relates to the power structure. Some don't especially want to see you wringing your hands in indecisiveness. They want a stronger leader. Others aren't impressed by your title or position; they want you to be their collaborator. Your interaction with each one should reflect the fact that you understand your employees as individuals—and that you respect them as individuals. Just as much as you hope they respect you.

- **Let people know where they stand.** Set clear and reasonable goals for your team. Make sure your employees know in real time how their performance is measuring up to not only your expectations but also those of their coworkers. Drive the feedback power throughout your team. Don't just bear the burden yourself.

Take advantage of mechanisms such as social media, texting, and online meeting services to help your employees tell each other how things are going. Keep in mind that younger employees might be actively interested in more frequent feedback, as well as more frequently updated career path planning. But don't assume that your older workers want annual reviews only.

■ **Spread the power throughout the team.** When you step down from the managerial pedestal, you allow team cohesiveness to truly set in. They will learn to rely on each other. Your goal as an engaging manager is to share accountability and drive managerial responsibilities throughout the group. Give your team the chance to identify and set the goals they need to meet to achieve corporate objectives.

When the time comes to take your team success stories up the org chart so that the rest of the company can model your example, don't tell the story yourself. Give that honor to your employees.

TRUTH

34

Trust is your strongest persuasion tool

If you've been in the work world long enough to be managing people, chances are excellent that you've been subjected to that classic trust exercise—you know the one—where you fall backward like a board, with every expectation that the person standing behind you will break your fall. Of course, that person is going to catch you. Everyone is watching.

Here's the real trust question: Would you depend on that same person to tell you the whole truth—even if that truth threatens careers? Or embarrasses your company? Or might cause key talent to quit? If you say no, you have a trust issue. If your people say no to the same question about you, you've got a big corporate culture, engagement problem.

Withholding critical muscle power and back-stoppage is frowned upon in those trust-building exercises. But withholding high-level information is too often tolerated in a larger cultural context. If it's okay culturally for you to keep critical information to yourself and not share it with your employees, can you really expect to persuade them to give the company their best efforts? Why should they? They're not trusting the business they work for, nor, by extension, are they trusting you.

To lead a team of individuals truly committed to giving their best and beyond to the organization, you must first answer this question: "What are my own priorities?" Too often, we see evidence of leaders putting themselves first over the company and their employees. This, says Tim Garrett, former CHRO of Honda America Manufacturing (which remains the oldest nonunion auto manufacturer in North America), is the first breach of trust in the cultural fabric of the company.

"There are three priorities of leadership, in this order: the organization, your people, and then you," he says. "What this really requires of you is that you have the courage to stand up for what you know is right, even if your position might directly hurt you politically.

"If you want to build a workforce that is truly committed and dedicated, they have to believe that you as a leader are someone who they know they can trust and that you will have their backs," he says. "You have to hold people accountable to the expectations of the organization. In return, you're obligated to provide your people with the needs and expectations they have: respect, honesty, dignity, fairness, equality. Which one of those elements is at odds with a company's best interests? None of them."

There are three priorities of leadership, in this order: the organization, your people, and then you.

Don't protect your people from the hard truths of your company's realities. They already know what's going on—in some ways probably better than you do, from a different perspective. They come to work, they talk to each other; those departmental silos that the executive team has worked so hard to soften and even dissolve have become efficient communications conduits.

Now what your people need to know is how much are you going to tell them? If you leave anything out—essential information that they already know—they're going to wonder what else you're not telling them. And can you blame them for imagining the worst?

"One of the biggest mistakes that leaders make is that they fail to realize that individuals are smart people," says Garrett. "This is their livelihood that we're talking about. They can look around and figure out what's going on—good and bad. When we fail to be upfront and honest with them (even if it's because we don't want them to be worried or upset), we're not being honest. And consequently, they're not going to trust us."

Full disclosure doesn't mean reckless indiscretion. "I can't talk about that" is also the truth. Employees know that there are just some things you can't discuss with your team (their own salaries, for instance). But they may not be fully aware of the limitations of what you can say and what you can't say. So, they might innocently ask you a question that's out of line. They probably don't mean to invade the boundaries of propriety. They just want to know what's going on.

By saying "I can't talk about that," you're communicating volumes. You're telling your people that you have limitations embedded in your own role in the company, that you are committed to giving them all the information you can talk about. And they can trust you—to not only share what you know to help them make smart decisions about their careers and the way they can help the company but also to keep their secrets.

TRUTH

35

If they aren't buying it, they aren't doing it

Over recent years, the wise thing has been to help employees see the connection between their work inside the company and their external customers' experience of their product. Southwest Airlines, of course, has been famously trotted out as an example of this *internal branding*. It gives its customers the "freedom" to fly affordably and enjoy life through travel. Therefore, the employees should feel the same kind of freedom to do their jobs well—and enjoy life on the job. With internal branding, all the *whys* of how they're expected to do their job are imbedded in the cultural conversations employees have with the company overall. Make the experience of doing the job consistent with the experience of using the resulting product, the reasoning goes, and you've got a better product (not to mention a stronger customer relationship and larger market share).

On an organizational, macro level, these kinds of conversations are driven via big campaigns coming out of corporate communications, marketing, and HR. But, as a people manager, you have the micro-level responsibility of making the same kinds of emotional links to the employees' daily deliverables. Marketing managers understand that customers are volunteers—they can always go somewhere else for what they need. Your employees are also volunteers—they can always go somewhere else for a paycheck.

> Your employees are also volunteers—they can always go somewhere else for a paycheck.

You're the ultimate brand manager—helping your employees connect the value of what they do in their jobs to the value of the jobs themselves. This isn't about engaging what you might have once considered to be their discretionary effort. This is about engaging the basic fundamentals of their job responsibilities. If your employees aren't fully engaged in the spirit behind the tasks of their days, they will do just the bare minimum and then sit around waiting for you to tell them what's next. In addition to telling them the *what*, you have to inspire them with the *why*. Do that well, and you've got employees who are sold on the mission of the day.

> You're the ultimate brand manager.

Your clout as the boss won't cut it anymore. "Because I said so" may have worked with a 5-year-old (once), but not with people who probably know their job better than you do. And, of course, you better forget about "my way or the highway." Just as you can't force a customer to buy, you can't compel a valued employee to perform. "My way or the highway" will result in just one response: "Yeah, okay." And it won't be the *okay* of compliance.

In today's daily workplace, your job as manager is to sell the value of the mundane as much as the marvelous. Your challenge is only as difficult as your customer (your employee) is resistant, or as easy as your employee is emotionally bought-in to the powerful value proposition behind the task.

> Your job as manager is to sell the value of the mundane as much as the marvelous.

Sell your employees on the mission of the job they do. Speak about their roles and responsibilities in terms of customer service. Help your employees see how their duties and tasks serve customers down the line—even if that customer is in accounting down the hall. An understanding of the entire value proposition of your department and how its function serves your business unit and the entire corporation will help your employees see how their daily efforts have meaning beyond the immediate sense of hassle and deadline.

And don't make the mistake of interpreting resistance as a demonstration of "no." Salespeople don't take *no* for an answer; neither should you. Find out what the resistance is based on and address that issue specifically. Lack of time? No money? Lack of other essential resources? Maybe your employees need to be convinced that their effort is essential? And do what successful salespeople do. They take that resistance as hints from the customer on how they can successfully seal the deal.

When you get resistance from your employees, don't punish them. Convince them to buy.

36

Overselling an opportunity can cost you precious talent

These days managers are probably more experienced in laying off valued talent than they are at hiring them. So, can you really be blamed for becoming maybe a little overexuberant when you have the chance to hire someone fresh and new? Just think of the possibilities!

That's the problem. Getting carried away with those possibilities could result in you having to fill that position all over again, losing your hard-found favorite choice in the bargain.

You know how the hiring lifecycle goes: After the initial thrill of hearing that you have the budget for a new employee, you lose a bit of that joy in the grueling process of writing the job description. Then you lose a little bit more of that joy when the first round of applications come in. And by the time you've interviewed your fifteenth candidate, your spirits are flattened to a flagstone. But then—cue the angelic choir and bring up the heroic backlighting—The One walks in.

The One is perfect. The resumé checks all the boxes. Better still, the two of you hit it off with an electrified chemistry that could only be described as scandalous. Ideas are flying back and forth like a world-class tennis match. And before you know it, in the high-spirited joy of having found The One, you've promised the moon. Well, at least you didn't exactly say no to the moon. And your new candidate—now employee—comes to work expecting, well, the moon.

And now you must begin the process of reeling back those promises. Which coincides with the process of losing that great talent you found.

> You might be brainstorming, but the candidate is taking notes.

Cathy Fyock, vice president of strategy services for the Kentucky-based HR consulting firm Hanna Resource Group, warns against going overboard with promises made that the height of excitement during the job interview. Even when you know for a fact you haven't made promises, they are being perceived and received by The One as promises. You might be brainstorming, but the candidate is taking notes.

"You are obligated to match the content of the job interview with the content of the job itself," she says. "People tend to think that the carrot that you dangle in front of a candidate is the formal compensation package. But the candidate is also seeing other attributes of the job itself as a major reason why they would choose one job offer over another.

"There's a temptation to pick up on the desires of the candidate without thinking through what those desires actually mean in practical terms to you, your team, and your candidate," she says. "And then you find yourself with a new employee coming to work on Day One with a kit of expectations that you have no intention of delivering on."

You're not entirely to blame. Conditions of modern-day job interviews set you up for expanding expectations beyond the formal, established boundaries of the open job requisition. In a knowledge-based job market, interviews take on more of an environment of consultative selling (where candidates set themselves apart from their equally qualified competition by volunteering ideas for solutions to your existing business problems). This creates a freewheeling conversation where you put down whatever script or checklist you might have and great ideas bounce back and forth.

What will the most desirable candidates likely want from this new job opportunity that you might not be prepared to provide once the job actually begins?

- Autonomy
- Company resources
- Cooperative organizational culture willing to transform as the new employee pursues a goal of *making a difference*
- Easy access to key decision makers throughout the organization

Is it reasonable to expect you to deliver on exactly the job opportunity described in the interviews? Yes. But let's face it: Job roles and responsibilities are liable to shift as a company transforms itself to respond to its own changing marketplace. These things happen. And mature employees recognize that fact of business life. When that time comes, it will be up to them to decide whether your company's needs and opportunities still provide a promising package for them. Or whether they should start looking elsewhere.

But being clear about the responsibilities and opportunities for the current job as you're interviewing candidates will give The One every chance to make a wise career choice and then get started on the right foot. Don't feel obligated to stick to the job req script in your interviews. But don't lose sight of the likely boundaries either.

This way both of you will make wise, informed choices. And neither of you will have to suffer through a new round of interviews again any time soon.

TRUTH

37

Focusing on what's right can help solve what's wrong

When you face a mandate for change within your department or company, you can choose two different approaches: You can obsess on the problem until you're limply depleted of ideas, or you can go the other way and obsess about what's going *well* and allow the power of positive focus to drive a constructive plan for the transformation you need.

Metaphysical theorists will tell you that whatever you focus on is the thing that expands. For a more managerial perspective, the late Peter Drucker, widely considered to be the founding father of the study of management, put it this way: "Leading change is about aligning people's strengths so that their weaknesses become irrelevant." Either way, the message is this: If you want to build positive change, sharpening your beam of attention strictly on what's wrong and needs to be changed is not going to motivate your team toward the better future. The ideal future is built on what's already great, highly functioning, healthy, and whole.

> The ideal future is built on what's already great, highly functioning, healthy, and whole.

If you want your team to work toward positive change in your organization, the practice known as *appreciative inquiry* can be just the approach you need for gathering your people into a workplace community of forward-thinking, mutually supportive change agents. In this approach, the task is broken down into five phases, all of which tap into your employees' creative attentions, strengths, resources, and assets toward creating positive change—which is a lot more motivating that trying to fix only what's wrong:

Phase 1. Frame the task in a positive, affirming way. Instead of asking, for instance, "How can we reduce this high turnover?" ask "What is it about this organization that inspires people to stay?"

Phase 2. Focus on what is great about the organization as it is right now. Lead your team into discussing in as rich detail as possible all those elements that make up your organization's positive *core*. Create an opportunity for your team to exchange stories about times they felt that the company was at its best, when they were at their best, and what can be learned and borrowed from those examples to catalyze the change that's necessary now.

Phase 3. Dream about what could be. Allow your team to brainstorm in as vividly as possible all the different ways the organization can improve to serve your customers even better. If there was ever a time to

Focus on what is great about the organization as it is right now.

indulge in "blue sky" thinking, this is it. There should be no limits to the grandiosity of the vision and ideas. The ideas should be as emotionally compelling as possible, without regard (at this point) to practical applications.

Phase 4. This is the practical application phase. The dreams take a significant step closer to becoming real in the design phase. This is where the emotionally compelling ideals are translated into processes, outcomes, decisions, and systems that will help the Phase 3 ideals actually take shape.

Phase 5. The destiny phase calls upon the participants to actually commit themselves to all the actions necessary to transform the dreams they devised into the realities essential for moving their organization forward.

The power of the appreciative inquiry approach to motivating change is drawn from the fact that all players are invited to participate within a positive culture of possibility. This is far more inspiring and motivating than the more traditional shame-based focus of determining what the root cause is of a problem (barriers, failures, resistance). With appreciative inquiry, possibility-based brainstorming is launched from the belief that the organization is already at its best.

All players are invited to participate within a positive culture of possibility.

It's human nature to be more inspired by improving on what's already great than in wallowing in the muddy trenches of what's going wrong. Make a point of reminding your team members of their excellence. And keep them in the habit of appreciating the strengths they bring as a group to the organization, as well as the successes that they have already racked up in their collective histories.

38

High performers are motivated by a piece of the action

Sometimes you have a star employee who has nowhere else to grow in your organization. Maybe this person is *the* member of a one-member team of uniquely needed skills. Maybe this person is next in line for your job, but you're not going anywhere.

Regardless of the reason behind this person's short dead end, you still want to hang on to this talent. Your star is beloved by your customers. Or there's deep organizational knowledge there that shouldn't be allowed to walk out the door. Whatever that star talent represents to you, you know that great opportunities lie for this person far beyond your organization. And you just don't want him to go.

> Whatever that star talent represents to you, you know that great opportunities lie for this person far beyond your organization.

What do you do? Here's what Brenda Helps did. As senior vice president of HR for Tucson's Miraval Arizona Resort and Spa, she has created what she calls an *outcome-oriented workforce*. Her solution is to retain extraordinary employees by linking additional employee effort with bottom-line results. For the employees, that translates into added incentive and rewards for improving their own value to the company. And they don't have to leave a great employer just for the sake of growing their careers. Here are two examples:

■ **Bringing real estate sales in-house**

A portion of Miraval's property is dedicated to privately owned villas. A full-time concierge gives the residents the same high service standards that the resort guests expect. She knows their needs, tastes, and preferences. She prepares the villas for them in anticipation of their arrival. She loves her work, but she is ready to grow to the next step. Miraval wants to keep her, naturally. But there was no natural next step up within the established organization. So this is what Miraval did for her: Miraval sent her to real estate school. Consequently, she was licensed to sell Miraval's two remaining available properties. And she sold both of them within 4 months. Who better to sell those properties than someone who knows and loves the program? And someone who will say to the buyer, "And, guess what! I'll be here to take care of you when you move in!"

Advantages: Instead of the real estate commissions going to an external agency, she was able to make those commissions herself—enjoying the direct rewards of her additional value as a licensed real estate agent. For Miraval, no one knows the villa program or is as personally passionate about the program as she is. So Miraval's interests were represented by someone authentically enthusiastic about the product and deeply committed to delivering the level of service Miraval's guests would expect.

She has also started a waiting list for potential buyers. (As the concierge for the villa program, she's perfectly positioned to know who had such a wonderful time as a villa guest that they would aspire to be an owner.) As a result, she's tracking the market demand for the villas and helping Miraval determine when the best time will come to build additional units.

■ **Sharing the savings on a reengineered telecommunications contract**

Miraval's director of finance has potential to spare well beyond his formally described job. Miraval recognized this, and he knew it too. Instead of passively hoping that he wouldn't start looking for a more challenging position elsewhere, Miraval looked for ways that he could earn more through additional revenue-building projects. First up: Reduce their telecommunications cost. The deal: If he achieved a goal savings, he would receive a commission. Success!

Employers have had to take truly rigorous steps to make sure that each position directly serves the vitality of the enterprise. At the same time, individuals have to take a hard look at how what they do more than just meets a job description—how they might actually add to the business strength of the enterprise. The high-value employees (the ones you want to keep, in other words) have had to take on the mindset of an entrepreneur to some extent. They know their value like never before, and they want to be rewarded for it in some way.

Think of these people as micro-entrepreneurs, and find ways that they can directly serve the bottom line above and beyond the call of their formal job description. Reward them for that extra effort and result. Think of yourself as a kind of talent broker—creatively combining micro-entrepreneur with a rewarding business opportunity. You'll be using your own value-add, entrepreneurial talents and energies to benefit your business's interests. Who knows? You might find *yourself* with a reengaged passion for the work you do. And your company will benefit from keeping you as well.

39

All the generations want the same things

In recent years—especially before the current economic crisis kicked in—clear delineations seemed to exist among the various groups we like to define as generations. Baby Boomers, GenX, GenY, and Millennials were believed to want different things from work, to have different attitudes toward their work, and to have different expectations from their management. Consequently, a whole management consulting expertise emerged designed to make business leaders feel uncertain about their approach to managing employees from different age groups—and then to reap the financial rewards from serving that organizational uncertainty.

What if we were all wrong? Economic stresses and a shrinking job market are turning out to be extremely effective generational equalizers. The previously smug Millennials are discovering what Baby Boomers experienced when entering an equally hostile job market back in the 1970s. The lesson: The world doesn't owe you a job, and there are no participation trophies.

There really isn't much difference between Baby Boomers and Millennials. Baby Boomers are, in a sense, just Millennials with gray hair (or touched-up roots in the never-ending quest to succeed in our youth-oriented culture). Baby Boomers, after all, originated the youth culture. Baby Boomers entered adulthood with a certain set of entitlement expectations that sprang from growing up in a time of relative prosperity and a weird kind of peace around the world. (Sure, there was the Cold War and the dive-under-your-desk threat of nuclear warfare. But really, as a generation, childhood was mainly about consumerism and safe, backyard fun.) Jobs were perceived to be secure ("go to college and you're set for life"), and it wasn't until Boomers were in their late teens or early adulthood that their parents began to lose their jobs in mass numbers. All the while, as a broad generalization, Baby Boomers explored what it meant to *question authority* and experimented with various degrees of unconventionalism.

Rules were questioned and broken. Until hard cycles of dreary economic realities of the 70s and 80s fractured the implied promise

There really isn't much difference between Baby Boomers and Millennials.

of work-hard-get-good-grades-get-a-job-work-hard-keep-that-job formula. Oops. Life's not fair after all.

It was at that point that Baby Boomers learned what their parents knew all along. And now younger generations are learning what the Baby Boomers have known all along. They entered the workforce full of so-called *new economy* positive expectations, expecting the economic trend line to be a steep vertical climb. Employers competed viciously with each other to attract and keep the most desirable employees (who are now called *talent*). There was title inflation, where it seemed that anyone who could fog a mirror could become a vice president or CEO before 30. And recruiters even tolerated the presence of Mom and Dad at job interviews. Whatever it takes to staff up and keep the company humming.

If you're a manager, it's still up to you to keep your company humming. It's your mission to manage your employees in such a way that you draw their best, most committed, most excellent performance from them—both as individuals and as a team. But maybe it's time to stop focusing on the differentiated expectations of generations and start looking at what everyone needs to give his or her best to their team and company: clarity of roles and expectations and to be treated with respect.

"We're all a function of our environment," says Robert Critchley, a human resources consultant in Sydney, Australia. "While it's important to have a general idea of how the different generations work differently, please take a moment to understand that GenY's are really no different than Baby Boomers when they were the same age.

"For the last 10 years we've been operating under the general assumption that GenY workers were more relaxed, more entitled about their work expectations. But now that they've experienced the realities of widescale unemployment, the struggles of finding a job and taking care of their families' basic needs, they're acting just the same as Boomers. Old, assumed expectations are largely obsolete."

Critchley emphasizes the importance of helping employees see beyond the immediately obvious category of what generations their coworkers happen to belong to and to learn to see each other as individuals instead.

"Establish a team culture of respect, and out of that they'll respect you" he says. "Be direct. Be flexible. Be thoughtful. Seek to understand them as individuals."

And don't typecast according to age.

"Be generation savvy, but don't be surprised when you meet a 60-year-old who behaves like a 30-year-old, and a 25-year-old who behaves like a 50-year-old," he says.

TRUTH

40

Compassion promotes performance

In the course of human events, work still has to get done. And unfortunately, we can't make ourselves so busy that we can hold off the normal course of human events. No matter how we cram our calendars with wall-to-wall appointments, our lives are still filled with the terrible happenstances of being human: death, illness, accidents, national tragedies. The more people you have in your department, the more you are faced with the need to rise above your own fears and feelings and extend compassion to your employees.

This can be a frightening time for you, too, even if you're not personally or directly affected by the tragedy. You risk saying or doing the very thing that will make matters worse for your employees. You want to be sensitive to their privacy. You want to give them time to recover from the shock of loss. You might even feel the urge to keep your distance to give them the space they need to take care of themselves. But distance from you can appear to be indifference to them.

Distance from you can appear to be indifference to them.

Managers petrified by the prospect of doing the wrong thing often give into the temptation of not doing anything at all. And that can be worse. The way you take care of your employees during this rough time will benefit you later as they recall your kindness, thoughtfulness, discretion, and loyalty:

- **Consider the context of the crisis.** If the situation directly affects multiple employees (a severe hurricane, for instance), consult with the corporate-level HR office to brainstorm ways you can respond to the urgency. You might be able to arrange for cash advances and loans to help employees secure temporary housing or even relocate to other company locations around the country.

    If the crisis is affecting only one individual, discreetly talk with that employee to explore ways that you can help.

- **Don't take "nothing" for an answer.** If you ask an employee whose head is swimming with overwhelm and panic, "Is there anything I can do?" Chances are you're going to hear, "Nothing, thanks." That's the easy, polite answer. Don't believe it. There's plenty that you can do. You just have to think of it yourself.

If the employee is intensely private or easily embarrassed, do something quiet, such as cutting that person a check to pay for a personal chef for a week or so. This way, nourishment is taken

There's plenty that you can do. You just have to think of it yourself.

care of while the employee is focusing on the emergency. If your group is a close team, work up a roster of volunteers who will share the duty of making sure the employee's kitchen is stocked with food and the house is clean.

If the emergency is beyond your reach to help with directly, do something symbolic but still meaningful and significant. If your employee's family was involved in a serious accident, for instance, organize a departmental (or even organization-wide) blood drive. Or if the employee is dealing with cancer in the family, adopt a related fundraising event as your department's number-one extracurricular project.

■ **Seek the help *you* need to know how to reach out appropriately.** It's especially important that all your employees know that you care about them. But it may not come naturally to you to open your own heart and show your emotions during this time of crisis. You may be the boss, but you're not God. You can't read minds or see deep inside the hearts of your employees. Reassuringly, you shouldn't be expected to, either. If you feel that you're over your head with your employee's issue or behavior, get advice and support from someone you trust in your organization, be it your own boss, HR, or your employee assistance program.

How you treat one employee in need will tell all your employees that they will be able to count on you should their own crisis come. And don't forget: It's entirely possible that *you* could be on the receiving end of compassion the next time. The culture of caring that you demonstrate with each employee in crisis can flow upward in your direction just as easily as outward throughout your department. Either way, the caring that your team experiences and expresses will bind them as a team of mutual trust and reliance.

41

A hot star can brighten
your whole team

Who doesn't want star performers on their team? They can ratchet up the excellence of all your performers. Assuming that they don't haul their ego into the workplace, like their very own espresso machine, they can inspire would-be stars who have gotten into the habit of leaving their A game at home. They can bring a certain level of celebrity to your entire company. And, let's face it, they can make you look fantastic.

Some stars expect star treatment. Some stars just want the trust and respect necessary to be left alone to do their work. Some stars will be courted by your competitors who know the value of their brand, perhaps more than you do. Some stars just like to work with colleagues who care about the mission as much as they do and who aren't threatened by the little extra oomph of passion they bring to the table.

Stars need a little bit of special handling. But it's worth it for your entire team. Keep them onboard with your group, and their influence will lift the performance levels of everyone who works with them:

- **Choose their immediate teammates carefully. Nothing will alienate the brilliance of talent faster than being yoked to mediocrity.** If you want to attract and keep high performers, make sure they have people of the same caliber to play with. Not that your high performers are necessarily talent snobs. It's just as likely, if not more so, that the mediocre talent will do what they can to diminish, dilute, demoralize, or destroy the contributions of your best employees.

- **Accept the fact that your most impassioned employees are likely to contribute to their profession or industry outside the scope, confines, and control of your organization.** They're curious. They're passionate. They're generous. They're energetic. They know that to be cutting edge in their field, they must bring out the sharp implements and do the cutting themselves (which can threaten the dull-edged folks on the status quo side of your enterprise). Give them the time and flexibility to be active in their professional community. They'll bring back the goodies they gather (new knowledge, skills, acquaintances) to you.

- **Accept the possibility that your high performers have to cultivate a fan base to do their work.** They recognize that to build their own effectiveness in their field, they probably have to build a network or even a following, which necessitates creating celebrity of one sort or another. It's not necessarily an ego trip (although it might look like that to the mediocrity cadre). It's a necessity. Still it can foster envy, resentment, and general peevishness among the rest of your workforce, who aren't as energetic about their careers but still want the attention swag your stars appear to enjoy.

■ **Accept the fact that your customers might love your star more than your brand. Or that your star *is* your brand.** Is that necessarily a bad thing? It can be if your brand is more important to you than your customer is. But there is still no getting around this fact: If you have a star who positively influences how the public experiences your company's product or service (by inspiring excitement and loyalty and excellence), what's it worth to you to keep that star onboard? What's it going to cost you when you lose that star to a competitor?

■ **Use the star's presence to inspire the rest of your team to excellence.** Your employees are *your* customers. They have, in a sense, hired you to help guide their career development. If you have a star in the group, recruit that star to share his or her brilliance and to foster opportunities for excellence from your B++ players. And then recruit your B++ players to do the same for the B players and so on.

> Recruit that star to share his or her brilliance and to foster opportunities for excellence from your B++ players.

■ **Don't play favorites.** Sure, star talent is hard to find. But whole teams of really great B and B++ players are even harder to build. A star who is toxic, mean-spirited, or who dismisses the team spirit out of arrogance is not a star at all. Bending rules for one that you won't bend for all will result in trust and communication issues among your entire team. They'll end up resenting your star player (further diminishing your star's effectiveness) and losing respect for you (completely undermining your power as an inspiring leader).

Employee engagement experts agree that an important key to keeping your top performers is to give them continuing opportunities to develop their careers. Your star players can be your best asset with regard to helping raise the potential levels of all your people. This might just be the most valuable service they'll give you.

TRUTH

42

B players are your A team

We all know who the A players are. They're the ones with the sterling resumés who track steady upward trajectories, starting with preschool. They've worked for your competitors and know all their secrets. They keynote the big conferences and get invited to the receptions that the riffraff don't know about—not even you. When they open their mouths to speak, everything grinds to a halt, even the factory floor, so that people can hear every single word. They're paid exorbitant salaries, as well they should be. They're quite the catch, you know. You're lucky to have them.

You know who they are, but you don't know them very well. That's understandable. They haven't been with your department very long. And, actually, what's the point of getting to know them anyway? They won't be with you very long either. They're on their way up. So, a last-minute lunch is probably out of the question. They're busy having lunch with your boss. Or a recruiter. Or your competitor.

If you want company for lunch, ask a B player to join you. B players, who are too frequently discounted as also-rans, almost-but-not-quites, are not only much better company, but they also make your business a much better company. If you're looking for glitz, you won't find it on the B player. The B player will never be on the cover of *Vanity Fair* or even at the parties. The B player is too busy printing the magazine, making sure each copy is an exquisite, delightful, crisp jewel, to aspire to being the jewel itself. B players are brilliant at what they do, so they don't need a spotlight to shine.

B players, in short, are the ones you can't do without. In the bright light flashing around the A players, the B players may seem like failures in comparison. Ho-hum, hum-drums. But that's only if you value aspiration and ego. Which, as a wise manager, you don't. You value steady, focused, dedicated work. Attention to detail. A big-picture understanding of the industry. A deep well of institutional memories. A rich network of long-standing relationships. Firmly ensconced deep inside their jobs, they're not exposed to the fights or flights of fancy that come

> B players are brilliant at what they do, so they don't need a spotlight to shine.

along with A players and their whims. They can take the idea-of-the-month and transform it into both strategy and tactic that will push the business forward. You won't notice what they've done, because they're busy working on the next project, not looking for the limelight.

B players, in short, are the ones you can't do without.

Don't get the wrong idea about B players. They're not losers. Some of them are actually A players on a breather—super-high achievers who saw what personal price they were paying dedicating so much of their lives to their careers and decided to balance their lives out a little better. Some of them really love their jobs and simply aren't interested in climbing the career ladder. Or they're attached to their team members and get their fulfillment simply working every day with people they like. Or they're proud of the company. Or they're proud of the creativity, accuracy, and excellence with which they do their job. And so they do it exceedingly well. And you count on them.

Some of them are actually A players on a breather.

But B players are also not martyrs or selfless saints. They need recognition and reward for the jobs they do. They just might not be impressed with the sparkly promises that you routinely dangle in front of A players. They may not be motivated by the potential of the next promotion in a new city that would force them to uproot their contented family. But they might especially appreciate more salary. Or a paid trip to that conference that will help them do their job better. Or a mentor who will help them identify and help them achieve their next career goal (that they define in their own terms).

B players are truly high performers. Make sure they know you notice and appreciate who they are and what they do for your organization. No one wants to be invisible. So if you are too blinded by the flashy sparkle of your A players, there may come a day when you realize that your precious B players have mysteriously disappeared.

TRUTH

43

High performers have enough coffee mugs

You're a high performer. You're proud of your work. You do it independently, and you take responsibility for its outcome—on good *and* bad days. Exactly how many coffee mugs do you personally aspire to own before you can feel truly recognized and appreciated for all your contributions to your company? The best guess is a nice, round number: zero.

And do you really need another acrylic doodad, even if it does have an engraved, gold-tone label with your name on it? How about a balloon with the word *thanks* emblazoned on it? Do those things really help you sustain your passion for your job? Probably not. Quality employees don't need junk to keep up their passion for the job. They just need to be noticed and appreciated for what they do. That's probably the way you prefer to be treated. And that's also how your employees like to be treated.

> ## Employee recognition and rewards programs can actually do more harm than good.

Employee recognition and rewards programs can actually do more harm than good. For instance, the nature of the reward or recognition itself speaks volumes about what kind of employee behaviors you want. If you want your people to act like children, give them toys and then expect them to be delighted—or at least act like they are. If you want your people to be self-satisfied with insignificance, give them trashy trinkets for the smallest amount of accomplishment.

If, however, you want your employees to be authentic, adult, and self-motivating about their responsibilities and expectations, be real in return about the sincerity and specificity of your appreciation:

- **Lavish the recognition; spare the rewards.** When it comes to intangible forms of recognition (we're not talking paychecks and pensions here), people want to be noticed for investing their individual efforts toward the big-picture mission. No one likes to be invisible or a number. Everyone has a name, face, and life story. Know your direct reports—and preferably *their* direct reports—by name. Know a little bit about who they are, what brings them to your team, and what their dreams are. And let them know you know.

- **When you do give tangible rewards, make those rewards specific to the person or to the accomplishment that's being celebrated.** Even a relatively "catch them doing something right" $20 spot reward should have significance that speaks to them personally. Challenge yourself to come up with specific ideas for each employee. That tells them that you pay attention to who they are in addition to what they're doing for you.

> Challenge yourself to come up with specific ideas for each employee.

- **Give them a gift certificate to their future.** Send them to a key industry conference, for instance. Or offer to pay for a college course of their choice.

- **Give them the chance to benefit the future of others.** Recognize them for their wisdom. Get someone to interview them about their secrets of success, and gather their collective advice and insights to share with the rest of the company as an internal training program.

- **Let people see that you're trying.** Person-to-person appreciation doesn't come easy for many managers. If saying nice things to an employee's face makes you feel awkward and vulnerable, your employees probably already know this about you. So don't hide it. Deal with it. Some managers who are struggling with this personal behavior challenge will put ten pennies in one pocket, shifting a penny to another pocket every time they express sincere appreciation to an employee. Just because you may have to force yourself to do it this way doesn't make the appreciation itself any less authentic. You are working hard to integrate this habit into your daily work life. And your efforts will be noticed. Your people might even recognize you for it.

Sincere appreciation is an essential part of a workplace culture in which people throughout the ranks behave respectfully and encouragingly to each other. This is a way of life, not just some program goal to meet. Your people will know if you're speaking from the heart or reading from a script.

It really is the thought that counts. So when you want to recognize your employees in a way that's meaningful to them, put some thought behind it!

TRUTH

44

Discipline deepens engagement

Is there anyone who truly enjoys the discipline process inside his company? Even when managers are supported with rigorous and detailed discipline procedures, they're still nerve-wracking for everyone involved. Employees in the hot seat know they're possibly one step closer to being terminated; the manager is at risk for losing employees who once showed promise; and even the rest of the department is watching closely. Will the manager treat the employee fairly, according to the procedures laid out in the employee manual? Will the team lose a friend? Will a hardworking coworker get the break he deserves? Or will a slacker be allowed to stay on the job because the manager doesn't have the spine to fire her?

Discipline procedures themselves are too specific and driven by local law to cover in this book. But you might find it reassuring to look at how formal procedures can actually support your company's commitment to all its employees. If you follow them consistently, correctly, and humanely, you will be sending the message to your team members that they can *trust* you to fairly sustain the culture of excellence that you are building in less emotionally charged ways. As much as fairly applied disciplinary processes serve to correct the immediate problem with the target employee, they also serve to reassure all employees that the system works for them, mainly to the good.

Be discreet in your disciplinary process. Don't share your thoughts and plans with the target employee's coworkers. When you gossip about the private affairs of your employee, there are at least three victims (assuming you don't count the company as a whole at risk because of a potentially actionable privacy breach).

> When you gossip about the private affairs of your employee, there are at least three victims.

The first victim is the target employee, of course. Whatever he's done or not done should never be held up as an object lesson to his coworkers. Suffering public shaming is in no one's job description. The second victim is you. By gossiping, you have sent word to your entire department that your team can't trust you with their vulnerabilities and flaws. Even the most unsophisticated employee knows that, as the boss, you're honor-bound to keep the private concerns of your target employee just that—private. If you must talk, take it up with your own supervisor, whose job it is to equip you with what you need to cultivate excellence in your department.

There is also a third victim—one we typically don't think about in the gossip daisy chain. That's the person who had to listen to you talk about his coworker. You could be talking about that person's friend, and now you've burdened the coworker with information and secrets he knows he shouldn't have. Unless this is truly an unusual circumstance (such as a crime that involves the employees directly), your discretion tells your employees the most important thing they need to know: They can trust you.

Stick to a process of fairness, which is precisely what the formal discipline process gives you. As already discussed earlier in this book, when employees trust the process, they will be more likely to accept the outcome—even if they disagree with it. When you apply your company's discipline procedures precisely as they are laid out in the manual, no one can argue that you were unfair. They might not like the idea that you punished—or even terminated—a popular coworker. But if they can see that everything you did was fair, they'll come to accept your decision sooner or later—and respect you for making a painful, but possibly right, choice.

> **Your discretion tells your employees the most important thing they need to know: They can trust you.**

People are only human. And almost everything that happens on the job speaks directly to their survival needs. So, as much as they may care about the person who just went through the disciplinary procedure, an essential question lingers in their heads: "What will this mean to me?"

Use the disciplinary procedure well, wisely, and kindly, and your actions will give employees this message: "This means that you're working in a department that takes your work and career extremely seriously. I care about your personal well-being. And I'm ready to go through the necessary pain to make this department right again."

TRUTH

45

You don't have to inherit the problem employees

Unless you spend your life exclusively in serial start-ups, with each promotion you'll probably be managing previously established workgroups. Their systems, codes, behaviors, and organizational memories will already be in place when you show up. And you'll feel like you're constantly interrupting a long-running conversation. One of those conversations will be each employee's past performance on the job. And some of those old stories won't be pretty. As the new manager, you have the blank-slate choice of deciding whether these are "to be continued" stories or fresh-start opportunities for both you and the problem employees:

- **Take the past in moderation.** Your predecessor may have had the record-keeping skills of a bio-nuclear researcher but still had gotten it wrong with your problem employees. The relationship could have gotten off to the wrong start from the very beginning for any number of reasons. There was a spate of lateness. A discourteous word passed between them in an absent-minded moment. Whatever happened, no matter what the employees did (good or bad), those events were evaluated through a negative filter. But now the past is past, and this is the chance for both you and your problem employees to get it right.

> But now the past is past, and this is the chance for both you and your problem employees to get it right.

- **In addition to your team meetings, have private one-on-one meetings with all your employees, not just the problem ones.** Give all your employees every chance to tell you how they feel about the team, the projects, the department, the company—but *not* about how they feel about each other individually. Learn what the collective frame of mind is like as a result of your predecessor's regime and what their hopes are for progressive, productive change. See if your problem employees feel the same way or have completely different ideas of what the team should be doing.

During your private meeting with the problem employees, let them know that you see their file shows some difficulties. (Unless they're both a problem *and* stupid, they're not going to be surprised.) Ask them what their perspective is. Keep the conversation as unemotional as possible, but hear them out completely. Let them do most of the talking.

- **Resist the urge to suggest that they look at the situation from your predecessor's perspective.** You can bet your new promotion that others have tried this tactic before and failed. You can also bet that the minute you speak on behalf of the past, you've joined it in their eyes.

- **Help them see how they fit into the overall team.** They were hired for a reason, most likely their skill sets. Brainstorm together the ways they add value to the group. They have probably been so focused on the exasperation of trying to perform under

> Brainstorm together the ways they add value to the group.

frustrating circumstances that they have lost sight of what's good about the team. They have almost certainly lost sight of how they fit in this team. And the team may have lost sight about what's good about them.

- **Collaborate with them on envisioning successful performance.** Come up with measurable performance goals you can agree on. Make sure they're compelling enough to truly engage your employees' commitment. Ideally, these goals should speak to their own values and definitions of excellence. Agree on what the penalty should be if they fall short of their commitment.

- **Ask whether they need anything special from you to stay on track.** If they have been laboring under the heavy pressure of contempt from your predecessor, they will probably be mainly relieved to know that this particular load has lightened up, thanks to your open mind. So, maybe they need a weekly or monthly check-in meeting with you to make sure you both feel that things are going well.

- **Mark small successes subtly.** Most "most improved" awards are backhanded compliments. Most people want to be recognized for consistent excellence, not for the journey they've been on. Your earliest meetings with your problem employees were private. So celebrate the subsequent small successes equally privately.

Don't worry, your team is noticing. With the employees formerly known as *problem* back on the team, everyone is getting a fresh start.

TRUTH

46

Performance appraisals are really about you

The irony is exquisite: The one time of year when you're most likely to feel at most risk of conflict and confrontation with your employees is also the one time of year when you're most likely to see eye to eye with them. This is performance appraisal season. And this is what you have in common with your people: You all dread it.

There's no wonder. Performance appraisals have never been an especially happy time. This is when managers and employees put (or bang) their heads together to review what went wrong last year and figure out how to make the upcoming year better. This kind of conversation comes with the potential of criticisms, accusations, denials, warnings, threats, ultimatums, even terminations. If you're as uncomfortable with the review process as your direct reports are, you can very easily lose control over the conversation, and then it becomes even more emotionally charged.

This is an opportunity to reconnect with your employees in a positive way. To engagement-committed managers, annual performance reviews offer teachable moments meant to inspire and align their employees with next year's mission, deepening a relationship of trust and mutual respect in the process. Whether your people emerge from their meeting with you either shaking or smiling says more about your philosophy of performance management as an engagement tool than it does about what kind of employees they are—or will likely be over the next 12 months (if they stick around that long):

This is an opportunity to reconnect with your employees in a positive way.

- **The review meeting should hold no surprises—especially unpleasant ones.** This is not an annual performance *ambush*. If your people need to improve or adjust their performance to meet your standards and expectations, tell them early and often (as promptly as you can without humiliating them in front of others, and as often as you can tolerate before deciding to terminate them). Your job as their manager is to help them be successful in their jobs all

This is not an annual performance *ambush*.

year long. So the more you dread the annual event, the more you should look closely at whether you're doing *your* job the other 364 days of the year.

■ **Use the meeting as a way to model excellent customer service.** In the context of your management obligations, your employees are your customers because, as we've already established, your obligation is to give them what they need to do their jobs well. One of those necessities is pitch-perfect behavior modeling. So treat them with the utmost courtesy and consideration all the time, but especially during the review process. Why? This meeting is their point of purchase with you. Whether it's explicit or not, one of the outcomes of the meeting will be their determination as to whether they want to continue doing business with you for another 12 months.

> This meeting is their point of purchase with you.

■ **Remember that this is a review, not a disciplinary action.** You can make the most progress by focusing on what the employees are doing right and well. This isn't to say you must sugarcoat the entire conversation, but focusing only on what needs to be corrected or improved will just provoke them into thinking they might be better appreciated elsewhere. Talk about the wins of the past year and explore together what made those events especially successful. Then brainstorm ways that the employees can repeat those successes—maybe even best them next time.

If you must request improvements in the employees' behavior or productivity, make your comments as concrete as possible. Abstract advice (such as "You must be more flexible" or "you need to show more respect") are too vague to be instructive, and they're confusing enough to damage the trust between you.

■ **Set your expectations high, positive, and inspiring.** And then you'll have some terrific developments to celebrate together next year! Those are results that you'll be able to bring to your manager when the time comes for *your* performance appraisal. Everyone will be seeing eye to eye on what excellence looks like in your department. That will say a lot about you and what kind of job *you've* done as a people leader.

TRUTH

47

New hires can inspire current employees

Everyone gets a little nervous when a new hire must be found to fill a new position, recruited, and then brought onboard. Naturally, as the person's boss, you want someone with the skills to do the job and the temperament to do it well—and preferably pleasantly. A personality fit with the rest of the team would be great. You're lucky if you're able to conduct team interviews, with everyone agreeing on who the first-choice candidates might be.

It doesn't always work that way. Sometimes you just need to get someone onboard to meet critical needs and get essential work done. Hopefully, your current employees will go the extra mile to fold the newcomer into the group and make the first few days, weeks, and months as easy as possible.

New hires come with their own baggage, though, good and bad. Who you hire and the way you go about selecting that person can make a huge difference in helping your incumbent employees decide whether the golden age of your team is over and it's time to look for a new job themselves. Or perhaps the new hire is actually an exhilarating breeze about to blow through your workplace. Maybe your current employees are freshly energized by the prospect of this person's influence and passion.

Who you hire can inspire the people you already have. In addition to considering your candidates' skill sets, ask yourself these questions:

> Perhaps the new hire is actually an exhilarating breeze about to blow through your workplace.

- Does this candidate speak passionately about the industry or profession?

- Can he bring fresh knowledge and perspectives about new markets and new ways of applying new methods and techniques to old problems?

- Does this person seem to like people?

- How does this candidate embody your own vision for your department's future?

- Does this candidate demonstrate to your people your own personal commitment to bring them only the very best of colleagues to work with?

Employees who work in a highly engaged team setting will welcome new colleagues as a chance for a fresh start with new opportunities for unexpected insights and learning new ways of doing things. Assuming your current team members are already passionate about what they do, they're going to look for that same quality in their new teammate. And the care and time you take in selecting that new employee (even if it's done unilaterally rather than via a team selection process) demonstrate that you're committed to giving them what they need to be successful on the job—and that includes quality coworkers.

However, you might be tempted to hire in a panic, especially in a labor-shortage situation. Where your team may be made up of people you once hired for attitude and trained for skill later, it's possible that in your urgency, you'll now hire for skill and hope that your team eventually helps the new hire correct the attitude problem. That's a false economy, and you're doing your entire team a disservice—including your new hire, who will know as well as anyone (and probably sooner than most) that it's a poor fit.

> Keep your standards high, even if it means that you must run understaffed for a little while longer.

When you started your journey to creating a high-engagement culture of strong, impassioned coworkers, you set the bar very high for everyone—for your current employees, for yourself, and for everyone you bring onboard in the future. Keep your standards high, even if it means that you must run understaffed for a little while longer.

Your people will willingly take up the added burden of the vacant position's responsibility, especially if the delay demonstrates that you care enough to hire only the very best.

TRUTH

48

Terminations are an engagement tool

First of all, let's be clear about one *big* principle. Unless your soon-to-be departed has been the cause of a SWAT team visit or hazmat suits or a scattering of black fingerprint dust, firing someone should never be an occasion for celebration. If you derive a dark, secret satisfaction from telling someone that today's their last day, you might want to consider taking on a new job. One that involves working with, say, plants.

Terminations are rarely a happy occasion. It's not happy for the ex. If he or she wanted to leave badly enough to actually leave, that employee would have quit first. It's not happy for the company. There is inevitably unwelcome expense involved: severance, legal, the expenses associated with making the original hiring mistake. And the expenses associated with recruiting, interviewing, hiring, and training the replacement.

Now that we have that little proviso out of the way, let's look at the termination experience from the perspective of how the process will strengthen your team, your employees' relationship with you, your company, and each other:

- **Make sure the way you terminate your employee is absolutely consistent with the law and your company's processes and promises to its employees (like a progressive discipline procedure that might be in place).** Most importantly, it's the right—and safe—thing to do. But additionally, it also keeps *you* on the job too. You won't have the chance to restore engagement equilibrium in your team if you've been fired yourself.

- **Terminate others as you would have others terminate you.** Your company's values don't stop when management decides it no longer wants an employee. All those lofty and publicly pronounced values that your company's leadership wrote in the vacuum of early and hopeful times are even more important now when conversations will get excruciating.

  Your soon-to-be-ex employee is going to walk out into the world and turn into a customer, a competitor, an opinion-maker, a gossiper. What tone do you want that person to take when discussing the company and the last conversation? The way you treat your newly departed before they walk out the door can make a huge difference for your company's reputation.

It's also important to bear in mind that the person you say "good-bye" to today could be the same person you want to hire back again tomorrow. It's not unheard of for companies that lay off talent one week to call that same person back a week later to offer another—sometimes even better—job. You want to have treated that person in such a way that they'll happily say yes. And wholeheartedly commit to the job rather than just begrudgingly use it as a stopgap while they look for opportunities in a company that will keep its commitment to its stated values.

> The person you say "good-bye" to today could be the same person you want to hire back again tomorrow.

- **Remember that terminating an employee won't terminate that employee's relationship with colleagues.** Sure, you might try to impose a gag order as part of your severance agreement. And, under pressure, shock, and anxiety, the employee will sincerely agree to a "mum" policy. But there's something about sustained staring into an extra large margarita glass under the sympathetic gazes of former coworkers that will loosen tongues. You're going to give them something to talk about. Treat your terminated employee in such a way that whatever is said about you will be as benign as reasonably possible.

If you can, make it acceptable and safe for your employees to keep in touch with each other (they will anyway, hello LinkedIn). Smart employees know that their network will be more dependable than whatever position they happen to be holding at any given time. It's that network that will help them string together job after job, ultimately forming a career path that has some sort of logical narrative. Your tenure as their boss is, itself, fleeting. You will eventually be folded into their network of colleagues. So by supporting their individual efforts to keep their networks and connections strong and current, you'll be building your own career power over time.

- **Remember that your employees are watching how you hold up the employment brand promise through the way you terminate unwanted talent and how you behave afterward.** Just because someone has left, that doesn't make that employee irrelevant to the commitment and passion of your remaining employees. Their own engagement might start to unravel if they observe you betraying the values and integrity of your team culture.

- **Don't speak negatively about your recently departed to your team.** They will conclude that you can't be trusted. They'll be gone one of these days themselves. And what will you say about them then? If you must speak of the newly absent, reserve your comments for either neutral or positive thoughts. You're not protecting the departed. You are, through your actions, demonstrating to the remaining that their reputations are safe with you.

TRUTH

49

Innovation begins with y-e-s

Leaders have long been in the habit of assigning the responsibility for being creative to the people whose job it is to deliver something new. So it's natural to assume that the most important whizbang, breakthrough ideas come from research and development departments, business development, or even customer service. However, as management experts are becoming increasingly fluent in all the benefits of engaged employees, they're discovering that breakthrough creativity comes not so much from people who own the job of delivering new ideas as it does from people who feel great about the job they own—regardless of its core function.

Breakthrough creativity comes from people who feel great about the job they own—regardless of its core function.

According to a survey conducted by the *Gallup Management Journal*, 59 percent of engaged employees strongly agreed with the statement that their current job "brings out [their] most creative ideas." The more engaged the employee, the more likely she will offer new ideas.

But wait! There's more! The Gallup survey also showed that engaged employees are more likely to be positively receptive to ideas offered by their teammates. Then, as if that wasn't enough, they also report that they "feed off the creativity" of their colleagues. So, the result is an upwardly spiraling dynamic of free-flowing creativity and positive reinforcement, which then generates even more free-flowing creativity. That culture of mutually supportive breakthrough thinking can appear anywhere in the company, ultimately benefiting the

Create a culture of idea generosity.

entire organization's bottom line, regardless of whether the idea is a new product eureka or a simple solution for reducing waste in the recycling area.

But this spiral has to begin someplace. In your department, that *someplace* had better be your office. To take advantage of this upward-spiraling dynamic of energized and original thinking, you want to create a culture of idea generosity. If you establish a culture where employees trust that their ideas will be respectfully heard, they will be more likely to approach your office with breakthrough notions and inspirations. Therefore, your office must be Destination Yes.

This is not "yes" as in "Your wish is my command." You're not a genie. This is "yes" to your employees' most pressing request: to be given fair, respectful, and open-minded treatment. When your employees can assume that they'll be heard, they'll assume it's worth their energy to speak up.

Assumptions are contagious, and your employees will catch their clue from you. Consider your own automatic assumptions about the quality of ideas that your employees are most likely to bring forward. If scarcity thinking, mistrust, impatience, elitism, and hide-bound allegiance to rules cause you to assume that your employees' ideas are a waste of time, your employees will assume the same. And your office will become Destination What's the Point of Even Trying?

Good ideas become great ones when they're safely bounced around a team of well-willed colleagues who thrive on each other's inspirations.

But the culture of idea generosity thrives within an office that has the reputation for being Destination Yes. Good ideas become great ones when they're safely bounced around a team of well-willed colleagues who thrive on each other's inspirations.

The Danish philosopher Soren Kierkegaard once wrote, "And what wine is so sparkling, what so fragrant, what so intoxicating as possibility?"

Only one answer comes to mind: possibility shared in the safe and trusted circle of colleagues who gather within a culture called "yes."

When that happens, the possibilities are endless.

TRUTH

50

Everyone can be creative

Creativity is an essential component to any department today. It's the key to differentiation that will make you stand out among all your competitors, no matter what service or product you're providing your customers. This might actually come as bad news to you if you're not accustomed to thinking of yourself (or your department) as the creative type.

Or it might come as even worse news if you've been wishing all along that you were creative and having been watching your competitors eat your lunch. If you've tried to train your employees to be more creative, you probably know this already: Creativity may be a discipline, but it's not a teachable skill. It's more of a *frame of mind* that allows people to be more receptive to making fresh connections

> Creativity may be a discipline, but it's not a teachable skill. It's more of a frame of mind.

of notions that result in breakthrough ideas. So you can't teach creativity, but you can nurture it by providing an environment that inspires and invigorates your employees.

- **Take your employees on "artist dates."** In her book *The Artist's Way*, Julia Cameron recommends that her readers (primarily writers and visual artists) leave their desks and easels and go out into the world a couple of times a week to expose their souls to fresh colors, textures, and experiences that will eventually find their way into their work. Similarly at Ferrari, director of HR and organization Mario Almondo brings the artist dates to his employees via the Creativity Club. During this special event, Ferrari brings in jazz musicians, painters, writers, orchestra conductors, and actors to show its employees how artists come up with new ideas and solve creative problems.

- **Dissolve your silos.** Cross-pollinate your potential for ideas by bringing in employees from different departments to work on problems and their solutions. The fresh perspectives that outsiders will lend your group won't be censored with the prejudice of "we've already tried that" or "that can't be done." Likewise, lend your people to other departments so they can experience the creative satisfaction of offering their ideas to other people's problems.

- **Give your people what they need.** The notion of starving artist is charming only in Puccini operas. Your employees need money, time, rest, play, positive reinforcement, encouragement, and guidance to stay energized, hopeful, and courageous enough to keep coming up with new ideas and approaches to old problems.

- **Make your people happy.**
yesterday. Researchers have discovered that breakthrough ideas usually don't happen at the peak moment of happiness. Instead, breakthrough ideas typically happen most the day after the subjects reported feeling especially happy.

> Breakthrough ideas typically happen most the day after the subjects reported feeling especially happy.

- **Find ways to help your employees remember the meaning of their work.** Harvard Business School Professor Theresa Amabile says, "People are most creative when they care about their work and they're stretching their skills." Never let your employees lose sight of the meaning behind the work they do. No matter what your employees do, if they do it successfully, they're making life better or easier for someone. So bring some of your employees' customers into your organization so that they can tell the story of how your product or service made a difference to them. When you make sure they don't lose sight of that fact, you nurture their potential for creativity.

- **Open your department to volunteers.** Mark Twain once wrote that the definition of *work* is something you used to do for love but now you do for money. From the phenomena of YouTube and Wikipedia, we have learned that the public's passion extends into even the geekiest of pursuits, such as building an encyclopedia. If an encyclopedia project can attract volunteers, surely there's something about your organization that can appeal to discretionary passion. If there is, open your doors to this group and let their energies infect your employees.

> People are most creative when they care about their work.

As the engaging manager, you're in a bind. You're responsible for generating great performance and products that result from creativity. But you can't force creativity. All you can do is provide an environment where it can thrive. How you go about that is a creative challenge with your name on it.

TRUTH

51

You stand between inspiration and implementation

It's one thing to have a department that generates ideas—especially great ideas—like a machine. It's quite another thing to know how to take care of all those ideas—even the bad ones. Nobody can reasonably expect all her ideas to be successfully implemented, of course. But your people deserve to trust that you will take give their ideas respectful consideration, no matter how good or bad they are.

Your people deserve to trust that you will take give their ideas respectful consideration.

As their manager, you are the only one who stands between their brainchildren and any chance they'll have for having those ideas successfully put to good use. You are the gate between inspiration and implementation. The question now for you is whether that gate is routinely shut or open.

Researchers of organizational creativity and innovation say that managers are the main reason why great ideas never see the light of day. There are several reasons for this. You may not know as much as your people do about their field, so you might not be able to assess the value of the innovation. As a result, you might dismiss the idea as being too risky, when it really opens a valuable channel for change. Or perhaps you built your own personal sense of stability and security based on a certain set of variables, and your employees' ideas threaten the end of a very comfortable status quo for you. Or the innovations break certain entrenched rules—ways of doing things that your organization has become attached to. Researchers call this phenomenon *goal displacement*—where the rules that were once set up to support a company in achieving its goals become more venerated than the pursuit of the goals themselves.

This isn't to imply that with managerial responsibility, you've become an idea-phobe, that you fear fresh thought. People rarely intentionally close their minds to new ways of doing things. It just happens imperceptibly over time. But this still doesn't relieve you of your duty of ushering great ideas toward the next steps of implementation.

- **Do a gut check.** It's possible that subconsciously your mind has been closing to the notion of original ideas—especially those coming from your subordinates—over recent years. Look back on times when employees presented you with ideas (good or bad). How do you typically react to them? Do you hear them out noncritically? Or do you immediately start looking for operational flaws even as your employee is still speaking? Do you worry that your employees might be taking up too much valuable time making sure that their ideas are bulletproof *before* presenting them to you? Do you find yourself routinely liking your ideas better than your employees'? If you're not clear about these answers, ask a few employees you both respect and trust to give you the honest answer. If you're not happy with their feedback, let your group know that you're committed to making a change toward more idea-friendly behavior, and seek the coaching or training that will help you get back on the right track.

Managers are the main reason why great ideas never see the light of day.

- **Sell the idea to the right buyer.** An employee has just dropped a great idea on your desk. It's passed your still-considerable menu of qualifications. Now it's up to you to put it into action. Evangelize it throughout the channels only to the people who will take care of it. Who is in the best position to push it along? Will your boss receive it as appreciatively as you did and find the funding for it? Or does it need to be beta-tested first, perhaps by your own team or by volunteers and rabid fans of the company?

- **Give credit where credit's due.** Your people still own the idea, even though they gave it to you. Make sure you tell them what the idea's status is as it's being pushed forward to implementation. And make sure everyone along the line knows exactly who originated the idea—whether it was a single individual or a team effort.

Your people still own the idea, even though they gave it to you.

You'll get the credit you deserve. As a manager, your job is to create an environment where other people can put their brilliance to work. As more ideas from your department are implemented, you'll be known as the person who leads creativity into reality.

TRUTH

52

Failures promote progress

Companies thrive or fail on the power of the next Big Idea. While we think we may have a clue about what is likely to be the next sensation for our market, the chances are that we'll be either surprised or disappointed with each new venture. It's rare that our vision unfolds precisely as we expect it will.

> It's rare that our vision unfolds precisely as we expect it will.

From your people's perspective, a lot of time, talent, passion, and ego are burned as fuel in the service of the Big Idea. Each idea is exposed to scrutiny, acceptance, or rejection. Some of those ideas are perfectly sound, with every chance of success except one: The timing is wrong. Other ideas are thunderously dunderheaded notions that deserve to be put down as discreetly and humanely as possible—with no outsider the wiser.

Still other ideas make it through to production and explode in a huge ball of embarrassment, high in the sky, large enough for everyone to see: your own boss, your customers, the media, your team. You may have some explaining to do to your bosses. But you also have a new responsibility to the people who work for you. At this moment, your biggest job is to ignore the bleating of lesser minds who are thrilling at your failure. Focus on taking care of your team. With your people, your job isn't to save face. It's to save heart:

> With your people, your job isn't to save face. It's to save heart.

- **Keep your voice down and your head up.** Apologize on your *own* behalf as profusely and abjectly as you want to. But remember that you're also your team's representative right now. Your job is to restore its dignity both as its representative to the rest of the company and within your group itself. No one on your staff is being paid to hear you rant and pound your fist. Keep your calm, and you will model the most important behavior for the rest of your employees as you, as a group, re-envision the future.

- **If you have to point the finger, do it in private.** Your team may do its best work as a group, but it's still important to keep in mind that it's made up of individuals who need to feel that they won't be publicly humiliated for taking personal risks or making mistakes. You may feel justified in your anger and frustration to make an example of a single employee who, let's face it, really deserves to be fired. If you do it with the entire group as a witness, the example you'll be making is your own. And your group will learn only that you can't be trusted.

■ **Recruit your team as consultants.** Conduct a postmortem of the failed project and confer with your team as if they were esteemed, outside consultants. They are, after all, the world's foremost experts on this particular project. They know better than anyone why it went wrong. Spend some time exploring the things that went right, as well. There's learning to be captured on both positive and negative sides of this story. Show your employees that you see tremendous value in the (mis)adventure, and they will move forward to the next project equipped with greater wisdom.

Such an inclusive postmortem will also return to your team a sense of ownership of the project. It may have been ridiculed and criticized to smithereens by outsiders, but what's left still belongs to your group. So as a group, your team should decide what to do with the remains. Maybe they just want to file it under "never again" and forget about it. Or maybe they decide to conduct a cautionary seminar on what was learned from the project, or write a white paper or article for a business management journal.

It's easy for success-driven leaders to celebrate victories with their teams. But those are short wins that don't necessarily result in deepened relationships built on trust. If you're committed to being a mission-driven leader of an engaged team, you see that even failures are an opportunity to reinforce your collaborative culture of energized, freshly motivated individuals who respect themselves, each other (and that includes you), and what they do.

How you handle this failure will tell them how much risk they can afford to take with the next new Big Idea. Your behavior will solidify your team as a group who survived a big—if bad—adventure, and their shared learning will teach them to work more smoothly together the next time.

TRUTH

53

People don't quit their bosses, they quit their colleagues

You have, no doubt, heard this maxim: "People don't quit their companies, they quit their bosses." No pressure or anything.

It could be that this is no longer true—if it ever was. According to Michael Haid, senior vice president of talent management for Right Management, people are more inspired to stay by the quality of who their colleagues are than who their immediate boss might be. So, it stands to reason that your own role as a leader and standard setter might have shifted in response to this change. Your role in getting the best from people is actually to create an environment where they get the best from each other.

According to the 2012 World of Work Trends study released by Right Management's parent company, Manpower, the power of individual choice, combined with a predicted "talent mismatch" and global technological advancements, is forecast to revolutionize the way companies source and combine the talent they need to achieve their objectives. One development that Haid reports on is that once that talent is found and combined into a team, the team is likely to remain intact while its leaders change.

"Talent is relying more and more on each other than on a particular leader," he says. "We're seeing a lot of leader churn in many industries in many parts of the world where teams remain intact while leaders rotate above them. They're saying to each other, 'We may be here 6 months from now, but our leader may not. So, what are we going to do to hold ourselves together?'"

As a result, Haid predicts that engagement in the very near future will be more sustained by the peer group and less reliant on their one-to-one relationships with their managers (that would be you). But while this might make you less directly responsible for team engagement over time, this trend will not let you off the engagement hook in terms of how your decisions immediately affect the collaborative culture of the community that works for you. Your obligations remain the same, even though your role might evolve.

Hire for team sustainability. The idea of hiring for cultural fit has been around for several years now—and so, too, one would hope, the discipline of equipping a team with the expertise and skills necessary to carry on without you should the bus with your name on it cross paths with you tomorrow. But now you don't have to have a date with destiny under the eastbound express to expect that your team could long outlast you. Make sure that all the talent components you assemble can thrive on their own and actually survive the influences and ministrations of any just-passing-through manager.

Reward collaboration instead of competitiveness. As long as you have your team intact, it's your job to create a culture in which they can trust each other and focus on their shared objectives. They should have each other's back, not be stabbing each other's back. The management literature from the past few decades is full of tips and games for squeezing out the last drop of high performance from people depending on your goodwill for their paychecks. Leave that trickery in the past. It's not guaranteed to elicit any added performance output that would make much of a difference to company value. But it is guaranteed to hurt feelings, demoralize essential passion, and sow distrust throughout the team.

Give your team the chance to develop itself as a unit. Your people know each other's strengths and weaknesses probably even better than you do. In addition to developing each employee as a freestanding individual

> **They should have each other's back, not be stabbing each other's back.**

on his or her own career path, think of the entire team as a micro-enterprise, with each player adding knowledge and ability to the whole. Work with your team to identify its strengths and weakness and who might be the best team members to develop to strengthen those weaknesses. Even consider sending some members out into the larger organization "on loan," so to speak, so that they can receive essential developmental experiences that will strengthen the team's abilities when the loaners return to the fold. Imagine how much stronger your entire corporation would be with that kind of exchange system in place. Silos would dissolve quickly, and cross-departmental, mutually inspired collaboration could enhance all operations.

Make sure that business communication is group-wide, not just one on one. Champion every opportunity for the entire team to brainstorm and share ideas and opinions in real time. Naturally, some conversations must remain private (such as individual performance reviews or disciplinary actions). But make those conversations exceptions to the general rule of the team spirit of everyone working and communicating together as a group—a group of colleagues who deeply trust each other and who inspire each other to do their best work.

TRUTH

54

Extreme pressure kills inspired performance

Faster! Better! Cheaper! Faster! Better! Cheaper!

Oh heck. Who are we kidding? Let's go for what really counts. Faster! Faster! Faster! Faster! Come on, people, let's *mooooove!*

Fast is good, right? Time is money. When you're fast, you're first to market. When you're fast, you can use that extra time to come up with more new ideas that will bring you first to market (again) with products that your competitor hasn't even thought of yet. Fast is lean, clean, sharp. Why, there's even a business magazine named after fast. So it has to be good, right? Who would subscribe to *Slow Company* magazine?

And fast is fun. It's a challenge that managers put before their employees every day to see if they can squeeze a little more productivity and performance out of those brains already laboring under ever-tightening deadlines. If time is money, speed is the game in which that money is won. But there's just one problem: As a manager, when you're playing with speed, you're gambling with creativity, quality, accuracy, and performance. When you lose, it shows up in digits on the NYSE.

For most managers, fast is where it's at. They think that creativity and productivity exercised under pressure will produce hard, sharp, clear diamonds of progress and competitiveness. But Harvard Business School researchers are discovering just the opposite. They have found that extreme pressure kills creativity and insightful thinking. The stress that comes from the modern fondness for fast usually results in lack of mental clarity, physical exhaustion, and even the death of passion for the project. People are the least creative when they are under time pressure.

> As a manager, when you're playing with speed, you're gambling with creativity, quality, accuracy, and performance.

Still, you've got goals to meet. And, as the manager, you have to find a way to inspire and motivate your team to work just beyond what they think might be their capacity—but do it in such as way that you don't burn everyone out in the process:

- **Keep your deadlines reasonable.** Those circles under your employees' eyes may not be for lack of vitamins or sunshine. They could be from lack of sleep and spirit. Your team isn't a success if its members are meeting their deadlines but paying for the accomplishment with their health.

> Extreme pressure kills creativity and insightful thinking.

- **Keep your deadlines real.** If you become known as someone who puts artificial heat under your employees by unnecessarily accelerating your deadlines, you will lose all your clout to motivate your team. You will have lost that precious currency that can take you and your team anywhere: trust. If your management imposes absurd deadlines on *you,* with the expectation that hardship trickles downstream, stand up for your team and say no. Not every stretch goal or production challenge is worth the pain of the game.

- **Give your employees the time and space they need to get the job done.** If the work is so urgent that it demands the accelerated pace, it deserves prioritizing. Clear your employees' desks of any other competing obligations until this deliverable is met. Cancel all regular meetings, scheduling only those that are essential to the urgent task at hand.

- **Fully communicate the reasons why this project is so important and why its speed is essential.** If you want your employees to commit their passion and energy to meeting insane deadlines, you owe them an explanation as to why. If they understand the urgency behind the mission, they'll be able to take personal ownership of meeting that goal. Communication like this takes time, to be sure. But if you're looking at this last point and thinking, "I don't have time to walk my employees through the reasons why," then you need to double-check whether there's real urgency behind your request or if it's just a habit of being in a hurry.

Real deadlines set and reinforce an atmosphere of trust and respect among your entire team (including you). But repeatedly applied pressure transforms your people into slaves of the clock or calendar rather than service providers to your customers.

The clock is your friend. Don't fight it. And don't make your people fight it either.

TRUTH

55

Creativity is a
balancing act

Some departments seem to have all the fun. Their walls are covered in bright colors, with pretty or funny pictures tacked up everywhere. Little toys sit on cubicle ledges, and shreds of bright bunting are stuck to the acoustic tile overhead, which bristles with pencils that have been flung up there (colored pencils, no less, certainly not that old standby Ticonderoga #2). Laughter rings out from the half-walls on a regular basis. It's like those guys have no sense of dignity. You'd think this wasn't an office so much as a kindergarten. What a bunch of goofballs. And that's the accounting department, for Pete's sakes!

When you see that kind of high jinks inside a company, it's easy to assume that those folks spend a lot of time goofing off. And they might. But goofing off is good. Playfulness has become acknowledged as an essential component to a company's most competitive productivity edge: creativity. Creativity is the economic engine that drives the present to the future. According to *Fast Company* magazine, "The explosion of creative thinking in the past century and a half or so is the main reason living standards have risen eightfold, market economies have outperformed socialist ones, corporations have become innovation labs, and work has become more interesting."

> Creativity is the economic engine that drives the present to the future.

Few companies can thrive today without some level of creativity or innovation. Whether it's their product or their internal processes, they need a regular infusion of what University of Chicago Professor of Psychology Mihaly Csikszentmihalyi calls *acceptable novelty*. It's up to the managers to make their departments goofball-friendly, even if it's only just a little bit. You just never know when the next great ideas will come. And from where—even accounting!

> It's up to the managers to make their departments goofball-friendly.

Creativity is indeed a mystery. To be the most effective at managing a creativity-driven team, you have to be willing to relinquish control and give into that mystery. It's a paradox, to be sure. Get used to it. The paradoxes surrounding creativity are just beginning. In his research on creativity, creative people and the concept of flow (for which he is most famous), Csikszentmihalyi came up with these ten paradoxes. Learn to hold them loosely at the same time, and you stand a good chance of creating an atmosphere where your people can do their best, most original work. That could be *your* most post powerful creative contribution—provided, of course, that you can control your need for control:

- Creative people tend to be physically energetic but needing periods of downtime.

- Creative people tend to have high IQs, but they also harbor a sense of naiveté.

- Creative people tend to express their discipline through playfulness.

- Creative people tend to enjoy wild bouts of fantasy while being firmly grounded in reality.

- Creative people tend to be both extremely introverted and extremely extroverted.

- Creative people tend to be both humble and proud at the same time.

- Creative people tend to be unconstrained by gender-role stereotyping, displaying both masculine and feminine characteristics and behaviors.

- Creative people tend to be both traditional and rebellious.

- Creative people tend to be both passionate about their work but coolly professional and objective about it as well.

- The work that creative people do exposes them to pain, suffering, and rejection. But it also gives them the greatest joy.

If, as a manager, you can look at this list and think, "Well, that describes just about everyone on my team," consider yourself both blessed and cursed. (Oops, there's another paradox.) You have people who identify strongly with what they do, who are willing to

To be the most effective at managing a creativity-driven team, you have to be willing to relinquish control.

go out on a limb for the sake of their work, who can be fun to be with (except for those times when they aren't), and know the importance of developing products and processes that didn't exist yesterday (and within the confines and rules of convention and tradition). You're cursed in the sense that you have to somehow corral all this energy and eventually have something to show for it that will impress the, shall we say, less-creative types further up the corporate food chain.

TRUTH

56

Open questions ignite inspiring answers

In his 1996 book *Only the Paranoid Survive*, Intel CEO and cofounder Andy Grove told the story of how in the 1980s, he posed the following question to his partner Gordon Moore, "If we got kicked out and the board brought in a new CEO, what would he do?" Moore's answer was quick and decisive: The hypothetical CEO would get the company out of the memory chip business. So Grove proposed that they "fire" themselves, return as their own replacements, and do just what the new CEO would do. So they did, transforming Intel into a microprocessor maker. And that's why today most of us have "Intel inside" on our computers.

Good questions help us do our jobs better. Journalism students are trained to write their articles based on information gathered by five fundamental questions: Who? What? When? Where? Why? (With How? thrown in for good measure; business journalists, of course, ask "How much?") Those are the questions that measure and report on the past—which is the appropriate task of the journalist, who isn't paid to change the future. The journalist's old bag of tricks is certainly useful in helping you identify and measure progress and failure to date. And it will absolutely help you decide whom to assign the credit or the blame. But it won't help you get out of the spin cycle of the past and fling off into an entirely new set of possibilities.

The business leader must ask the question that springboards change. And that's the question that Grove posed to Moore: "What if?"

The question "what if" will help you open a variety of doors to different versions of the future. When Moore answered Grove's "what if" question, for instance, Intel marched into an entirely different destiny. "What if" is your essential tool for reinventing your organization, reassessing your current circumstances using a more forward-looking set of variables, opening your mind to alternative interpretations of current circumstances, realigning your employees to a new vision, and rededicating everyone's passion to a new mission.

> The business leader must ask the question that springboards change.

Here are some "what if" questions to try when you're ready to slough off the same old set of problems and take on an entirely new challenge:

"What if" is your essential tool for reinventing your organization.

- What if there's a better answer?

- What if there's a simpler approach?

- What if there's an entirely different way to interpret the meaning behind this problem?

- What if this failure is actually a great solution to a different problem?

- What if there is more than one solution?

- What if my team was given the chance to rehire me tomorrow?

- What if they could fire me instead?

- What if all my employees had to reapply for their jobs tomorrow?

- What if my employees met our customers face to face?

"What if" questions can be decidedly uncomfortable, especially for leaders who are most at home in realms that they can measure, schedule, and evaluate. The ambiguous landscapes of hypothetical thinking might cause you to worry—hypothetically, of course— "What if I'm asking the wrong question?" or the dreaded "What if I'm wrong?"

The beauty of the open-ended "what if" question is that there is no right or wrong answer. It's an invitation to be wise, to experiment, to see things a different way. To maybe, even, chuck the old business model and take on a new enterprise that will carry you further into a more prosperous future.

What if your "what if" turned out to be a good thing?

57

Serving your employees means managing your boss

Before you became a manager yourself, your line of responsibility was pretty straightforward—it was up. If you were lucky, you only had one boss. If things got complicated, you had multiple bosses. But they were still above you on the organization chart. And, ideally, if they had competing demands for your time and focus, they could work it out among themselves before coming to you with it.

Now that you're a manager yourself, you've got bosses all around you. Your philosophy of engagement requires you to take the position that you work for your employees—always making sure they have what they need to do their best work and caring about them personally.

There could be times when your boss gets in the way of your people doing their best work. If so, you've got an unruly boss. And it's up to you to fix that. So here's the paradox. In the service of working for your employees, as their manager, you sometimes have to boss your boss—preferably without getting fired.

> You sometimes have to boss your boss—preferably without getting fired.

Even without meaning to, unruly bosses can make your team's life miserable in so many ways:

- They impose a pile of conflicting priorities on your group, frustrating their efforts to make any progress on even a few of them.

- They withhold the necessary resources to get essential work done.

- They are unreliable with commitments.

- They alienate your team from you by making you look ineffectual.

- They make them feel undervalued and disrespected by giving them inappropriate projects.

- They make them feel that they are serving him rather than working for the company's big-picture purpose.

There is no simple solution to dissolving the effects of unruly bosses, especially if you work in an organization that's not completely committed to cultivating an engaged workplace. It can, in fact, ultimately prove to be impossible. But bosses are just as obligated to take care of their people (you, for instance) as you are obligated to take care of yours. So, it's reasonable to assume that they at least see the benefit of exploring ways you can work together to make the most of your team's passions, energies, and talents.

There's no getting around this. A meeting with your boss is in your immediate future. Call it yourself. That way you have some chance to control the agenda.

Check your own assumptions before going in. Are some of your own issues triggered by some personal, emotional conflicts with authority figures? Are you assuming your boss is just a jerk who doesn't care about your team? Or a spineless person who can't say no to her own boss? Is your problem a perceived lack of respect? Or a fear of conflict that your boss will stop listening to you the minute you bring up this touchy subject? You could be right on all those counts. But it's not your job to judge or psychoanalyze your boss. Your job is to help your boss find a way to help you serve your team, even if it means changing certain disruptive behaviors.

> Your job is to help your boss find a way to help you serve your team.

Assume only one thing: a collaborative stance. If you're working for a company committed to engagement, you can count on the fact that your boss is under pressure from above to help you do your job well. If your team's performance is measured by numbers and those numbers are slipping, you both know it—as does the leadership up the organizational ladder. So you're both responsible for improving performance. Now you have the basis for a discussion about partnering for performance improvement.

> You're both responsible for improving performance.

Speak to this mutual need to reframe the rest of your conversation as one between collaborators rather than between master and servant.

Be specific about what your team needs to do its job well. More time for each project? Assignments that are more appropriate to employees' skills, interests, and talents? A clear, unshifting set of priorities?

In return, find out what your boss needs from you. Maybe a weekly report will provide reassurance that everything is on track. A phone call might be all that's necessary. Or a spreadsheet would show at a glance that your department is already working at capacity on very important projects. That spreadsheet, by the way, could help your boss make a case to the leadership up the ranks that your department deserves more resources and fewer assignments—at least for the immediate time being.

You could be doing your boss a favor with this meeting. It's possible that she's been worrying about how to tell her boss to back off and let her do her job. And you've just modeled a way for her to do it.

TRUTH

58

Bad news is good news

We might have gone a little overboard in our efforts to create workplace cultures of empowered employees expected to solve all their problems by themselves. True—a dependent employee is not very productive to have around. Leaders don't like to have their concentration fractured all day long by little shards of complaints and petty roadblocks that their employees can easily dissolve on their own. It's one of the manager's responsibilities to encourage employees to take on challenges independently. You grow your organization by growing your people. And that means often making them do more than they think they can.

But you also have to know what's going on in your department. Making your employees solve all their problems independently can do serious damage to the company. You don't find out what's wrong before the problem gets too big to fix (or before it goes public). The solutions are limited only to those your employee can think of all by herself—that self-same employee who might have been the one to cause the bad news in the first place. You miss the chance to put the whole team behind a potential emergency.

> Making your employees solve all their problems independently can do serious damage to the company.

The problem is that, as the manager, you're the best one to distinguish between what's essential and what's insignificant. But you can't make that judgment unless you know it all. So you must be willing to hear it all. And to that end, oddly enough, the more bad news you hear, the happier you should be about it. Management's full of ironies, isn't it?

Your behavior should never make people afraid to bring you bad news. Bad news is fearsome enough without your people shouldering the added burden of worrying about how you're going to react to it. Are you inclined to yell? Make things bigger and more dreadful than they really are? Do you immediately look for someone to blame? Do you make a big, guilt-trippy show of blaming yourself? Do you punish the messenger? If you do, don't expect to hear anything but the happy stuff.

So, your team has shared the dreaded news with you. And now you have it. Knowledge is power; now go do something with it. It doesn't mean you have to own it all by yourself. You can still make the solution a learning experience—for your entire group, if not just for an individual employee. The experience of arriving

The more bad news you hear, the happier you should be about it.

at a solution as a team effort can be a bonding project in and of itself. No single employee may have the entire brilliant answer to the problem—particularly if it's an especially complex one. But a group focus can bring up group brilliance without necessarily blaming and shaming the individual who has brought it to the table.

The solution isn't the only learning here. The even-tempered way in which you handle the bad news is a teachable moment in and of itself. It's easy for your employees to trust their boss when everything is going swimmingly. But when someone has made a terrible mistake, all eyes will be on you to see how you react. This is your chance to teach your people that their trust is well placed with you, and that the way you are treating them is precisely the way you expect them to treat each other (and their own direct reports) should they be on the receiving end of bad news one of these days.

If you receive bad news on a regular basis (not a *frequent* basis, hopefully, but a relatively regular one), you can be pretty sure you're getting the whole story—or one

You can still make the solution a learning experience.

that's close to it. This is your chance to demonstrate to your people that they can trust you with the trouble as much as they can with the celebrations. Keep your temper, resist the urge to blame (at least in front of the entire team), focus on the solutions, and walk your employees through the problem-solving experience.

Assuming that your company isn't involved in a colossal, cross-functional, systemic scheme of fraud and malfeasance, there's a solution to almost any problem that your team can bring you on an average daily basis. You don't actually have to say "thanks" to them when they bring you breaking news that will throw your department into a momentary tailspin. But in the privacy of your own thoughts, you'll be able to say to yourself, "Today was a good day."

TRUTH

59

Trivial conversations
are essential

There are those who will complain that cubicles are counterproductive because they give employees little privacy. They need the chance to lose themselves in thought. To process the ideas that came up in the morning's meeting. To practice the new software uninterrupted. To call their mortgage broker. To check their bank account online. They don't need to be overheard or snuck up on. (You know those little mirrors stuck to the frame of monitors throughout your company? Those aren't vanity mirrors; they're rearview mirrors. Who would have ever predicted that one day we'd be driving our desktops with the help of rearview mirrors?)

There are still others, though, who will tell you that there's still too much isolation at work. Every single cubicle in the rabbit-warren of workspaces represents a lost opportunity to share ideas and spontaneous strokes of genius that will propel a project forward. We were trained as schoolchildren that there will be no talking. (Some children were better trained than others, of course.) And, since the classroom was basically our first workplace, we took our behaviors with us as we graduated from the world of laminated beech desk-and-chair combos all in a row and moved into the world of upholstered walls all in a row. The workday has begun; we must all be good children and be quiet now.

The workday has begun; we must all be good children and be quiet now.

Sure, you may have formal meetings during which everyone is expected to deliver updates, reports, and analyses. But much of the real work gets done on-the-fly—in the hallways, by the elevators, in the lunchroom, by the photocopier while waiting for the guy to please come and unjam the blasted thing.

As the manager, you hear all this undisciplined yakking from outside your own workspace and get this maddening feeling that maybe your department is out of control. But you should welcome that happy chatter—even if it's about such trivia as who won last night's reality show sensation. More work is being done through sharing inconsequential chitchat than you might realize.

Essential data is being exchanged during these seeming wasted idle moments:

- Who can be trusted?
- Who can open doors and facilitate otherwise hard-to-get meetings?
- Who can evangelize your project to the right people?
- Who will lend a consoling ear in moments of panic or crisis?

Essential data is being exchanged during these seeming wasted idle moments.

- Who has the to-die-for PDA filled with personal phone numbers of essential people?
- Who can influence the leadership decisions?
- Who happily pitches in on last-minute crunch deadlines?
- Who sees the bright side of just about any kind of problem?
- Who will suck the light right out of the sky with negativism?
- Who is an electrifying brainstormer?
- Who do you need to hide your wallet from?
- Who can fix that damned copier?

If you were to actually listen in on those conversations, you may not actually hear the words *copier, project, PDA, leadership.* You may instead hear the words *Emeril, can you believe?, sale, CNBC, Larry King, marinade, monster truck, immunity challenge.* But don't let that upset you or drive you to enforce a restriction on talking in the halls.

What you're really listening to is a conversation about trust, creativity, teamwork, process, and progress.

TRUTH

60

The way you listen speaks volumes

The trouble with running an engaged workplace is that people actually care about their work and what happens to the company. And when they care like that, they're going to get mad sometimes. The other trouble with running an engaged workplace is that you probably have some sort of open-door philosophy. Which means, by gum, when these people get mad, they're going to march right through that open door, plunk themselves down in a chair, and unburden themselves.

This is actually an opportunity for you. A meeting with an angry employee is your chance to demonstrate your commitment to your people:

> A meeting with an angry employee is your chance to demonstrate your commitment to your people.

- **Silently congratulate yourself that your employees are venting to _you_.** You may not necessarily like what you're hearing. But at least you're hearing it. It takes a lot of nerve (and trust) to unload on someone who has the power to say, "Well, then, perhaps you might be more happily employed elsewhere." The fact that they have muscled up the gumption to come to you with their problems demonstrates that they still hold the expectation that you at least care and are maybe able to do something about their issues. (Actively disengaged employees have long ago given up venting. Now they just tell their friends and maybe indulge in a little office thievery or vandalism. So if you're not getting visits from peeved employees now and then, that's the time to really worry.)

- **Don't expect them to be reasonable, rationale, or logical.** They might have rehearsed their speech before friends before coming to you. They might have made a list of grievances and points they hoped would keep them focused and unemotional. But all that could go right out the window if they're especially wound up. Assuming this is a rare incident and they are otherwise calm, cool-headed professionals, let it go. Unless they threaten you with bodily harm (in which case, call security), let them let 'er rip.

- **Listen hard.** Don't speak until they have had their complete say. Listen to what they are really trying to tell you inside the torrent of words and frustration. Look them in the eye while they're trying to express their resistance or fury. No matter how confused and confusing they may be, there's something buried in what they're saying that you need to know. If you focus on just hearing them, rather than talking back, you'll be able to keep your own calm and reason through this potentially stormy moment.

> If you're not getting visits from peeved employees now and then, that's the time to really worry.

- **Make sure you get it right.** When they're done, try to rephrase what you think you heard in your own words, and ask them if you understand them correctly. Give them a chance to refine their thoughts or revise your words to more accurately reflect their points. If they get wound up again and start repeating themselves, calmly say, "I think I've got it, thanks."

> Let them let 'er rip.

- **Calmly ask additional questions for clarity.** Ask them if they have any solutions to the problem in mind. Do they see a better way of approaching the problem? Or a better, more appropriate person to assign the troublesome project to? Is there anyone else they want you to talk to for confirmation or additional data?

- **Promise them only one thing.** That you'll get back to them and when. Don't be surprised if they try to push you for more definitive action. If they have worked for untrustworthy managers before, they might take "I'll get back to you" as manager-speak for "You've had your say. Now get out." Reassure them that you will get back to them, reminding them that a matter this important deserves some time to think through.

- **Keep your promise.** Better yet, surprise them: Be early. No matter what you do, even if you have to disappoint them with your final decision, keep the date you promised. And if you can, beat that date by a few days.

People coming to you with issues or complaints also bring with them lots of history of how their managers have let them down in the past. How you actually resolve the issue at hand may satisfy them. Or it might not. But the way you listen to everything they have to say about the matter and respectfully take action on it will take you far in solidifying the bond of trust between you.

The result: Everyone's expectations and hopes for the future will be raised significantly.

TRUTH

61

Crap happens

Unless you work for a waste management company, not much money gets made cleaning up the past. The real profits come in creating better ways of enjoying the future. That's the fun part, and fortunately, that's what most of us get paid for. But, as a manager, you're also paid for hanging in there—and inspiring your employees to stay on the team—when things don't go quite as you had expected.

Terrible things happen in business, even on an average day. Key clients go belly-up. An eleventh-hour investor loses his focus on your starving business because of a family emergency. Your main competitor steals your publicity thunder with a new product announcement that makes your latest offering look like last year's shoe style. These things happen. Your employees are naturally demoralized, and they're wondering, "What's the use of trying?" You can see it in their eyes.

For the moment, at any rate, your employees are feeling that maybe they're not the masters of their destiny after all. In the 1970s, psychologist Aaron Beck identified three interpretations of what happened that feed this feeling and lead straight to depression. They reflect a person's way of making sense of what just happened in terms of negative things he thinks about himself, the future, and the world in general: "I'm worthless," "the future is hopeless," and "this just goes to show there's never any point."

> You have to hang on to your own optimism for dear life.

When your business has hit a rough patch, this is your time to really show what you have as an engaging manager. You have to hang on to your own optimism for dear life. And you now have to back up your positive outlook with a powerful resiliency toolkit:

- **Return control to your team.** Help team members find a way to reconnect what they do to making some kind of difference in the world. A group project that makes an immediately visible difference will start to return them to their own sense of empowerment. This is not an elective. They can choose the project itself, but no one gets to sit this one out.

- **Return a sense of purpose to your team.** The fun of going after a potential win is always compelling. But even if the win is lost, there is still an underlying value or mission that hasn't changed. As a group, discuss the reasons why you embarked on this adventure in the first place. And restore a team commitment to the core meaning behind all the work you're doing.

- **Review your marketplace and its needs.** Your people are being paid to be change agents, but failure might have put them into a temporary existential shrug. Let them say, "Well, I guess that's just the way it is," only once, so they can get it out of their system. Then put them back on the job to understanding what their customers continue to need but still aren't getting.

- **Keep things in perspective.** You've had better days, to be sure, and your team has as well. But we've all had far worse days in recent years, personally, economically, and nationally.

- **Hang on to your own self-esteem.** The failure may have been your stupid idea in the first place. And now you're questioning your own abilities to make prudent decisions and wise business choices. Cut yourself a break. If you're not pushing your own personal boundaries as a leader, you're not letting your people know that it's okay for them to take calculated risks for the sake of your organization. Some work, some don't. That's life.

> If you're not pushing your own personal boundaries as a leader, you're not letting your people know that it's okay for them to take calculated risks.

Apologize to your team, if appropriate. Explore together what the team learned (good and bad) as a result of this misadventure. Acknowledge your group for their heroic dedication to the goal, and personally thank the individuals for their contributions to the effort. Be specific, one employee at a time.

Then get on with the next project. The future is waiting. The world deserves it. And you're up to the challenge.

TRUTH

62

Engaged employees
need to know more

When employee engagement is driven throughout the company as an organization-wide initiative, the corporate communications (corp comm) office almost always gets in on the action. In fact, because communications is such a core element to engagement, employee engagement is often driven by the corp comm office. For companies that see the value of sending corporate engagement messages and information throughout the ranks, this makes obvious sense. (It makes even better sense, however, when the HR and organizational effectiveness departments are allowed to collaborate with corp comm as equal partners in the initiative. As companies get increasingly sophisticated in understanding all the complex facets of employee engagement, corp comm will eventually *support* HR and organizational effectiveness, rather than lead it.)

Because employee engagement promotes a sense of ownership among engaged employees, they have a compelling need to know what's going on throughout the company. They have a stake in the outcome of the company's various projects, so they deserve to know how their efforts are paying off. Engaged employees take their roles inside their company very personally. So, they want to know how the company is being perceived by the community and in the media. They want to be reminded of what makes their job at their particular company better than their job at a different company.

This isn't a sense of entitlement that they expect to be catered to. They're pouring their passion and lives into their work. Therefore, they deserve to know what's going on throughout the entire company. And corp comm is there to make that happen.

> This isn't entitlement; they deserve to know what's going on.

Let's say you don't have the services of a communications department specifically dedicated to unifying all your company's employees through a common channel of messaging. Suppose that you're on your own. You can still keep your employees in the know. You'll just have to do it yourself:

- **Make a point of letting them know every single detail you can about what and how the business is doing.** Obviously, you'll be under some restrictions now and then—a planned merger, for instance, that can't go public until the companies are ready for it to go public to everyone. But it's a safe bet that companies generally can tell their employees much more than they do. Most of the time, it's simply an oversight. You don't have to make that mistake. Develop the habit of asking yourself if each and every development that crosses your desk is something that you can share with your people.

- **Tell them before they can find out any other way.** Don't let your employees get essential company news from the local television, their neighbors, or their stock broker. If the buzz is big enough to hit the grapevine, make sure your employees are among the first to find out from you.

- **Answer all questions fully and honestly.** If you want to nurture a workplace culture of individuals who own a stake in the company's success, they need to know that they can trust you for the straight scoop. Don't try to sugarcoat bad news. Tell it exactly as it is.

- **Give them room to speak freely.** Communication works only when it works both ways. Give employees the chance to speak freely within the circle of your department without fear of reprisals. This way, you'll know what's on their minds. You'll have the chance to respond to all their concerns. And you can correct misconceptions.

> If you want your employees to give their all to their jobs, you must be willing to give your all to them.

Engaged employees are high maintenance when it comes to requiring all the news and facts about their company. Can you blame them? They're being asked to provide their utmost of dedication, inspiration, and energy to their company. And over the years, they've seen examples of trust that was misplaced, with employees coming out the worse for their dedication.

If you want your employees to give their all to their jobs, you must be willing to give your all to them—especially all the company information that's fit to share. That way, they'll be better positioned to make informed, adult decisions—one of which, preferably, will be to stay and continue giving their all for the company.

TRUTH

63

Absence makes the employee happier

It was never funny, even when it was new. But somehow this joke experiences a magical rebirth with every new generation of managers who think they're amusing: The manager walks by an employee deeply concentrating on work and says, "You working hard? Or hardly working?"

But what if the employees are hardly ever there? What's a manager to do then? Whatever you do, don't bug them via Instant Message. According to the study "Why Teleworkers Are More Satisfied with Their Jobs Than Are Office-Based Workers: When Less Content is Beneficial," the authors discovered that the ability to work in peace outweighs any advantages that onsite employees might enjoy, such as picking up the whisper of a career-boosting rumor floating in the halls or engaging in interoffice skullduggery. Authors Kathryn Fonner (assistant professor of communication at University of Wisconsin – Milwaukee) and Michael Roloff (professor of communication studies at Northwestern University) found in their research that job satisfaction actually increases when personal interaction decreases.

The ability for individuals to telecommute will continue to enhance companies' ability to perform at high levels—expanding and contracting as necessary to achieve their objectives. Once you can accept the idea of employees working remotely, your small local operation can suddenly expand to a national, if not global, enterprise. A kitchen table in San Jose, California, can suddenly make a New York consulting operation a bicoastal enterprise. Add to that mix the population of independent contractors, virtual assistants, and freelancers available around the world, and you're a 24/7 operation spanning the globe.

> A kitchen table in San Jose, California, can suddenly make a New York consulting operation a bicoastal enterprise.

So, how do you manage all that scattered talent—with at least partial focus on keeping them by making sure they're engaged?

Upgrade your ideas around your own work. You are not a by-the-hour manager making sure your employees are 100% focused on company business during clock-in time. You are a by-the-project or by-the-objective manager. So it really doesn't matter what your telecommuters are doing at 2:30 p.m. And it doesn't matter what they're doing at 2:30 a.m. Your job is making sure that business objectives are met on time, not what time it is. This will make your conversations with your telecommuters much more satisfying for both sides.

Learn to love the online meeting services like Skype, Zoom.us, and GoToMeeting. You can hold team meetings online with no one leaving his or her desk—whether those desks are down the hall or Down Under. These services offer best-of-all-worlds advantages in that there is face-to-face interaction but no one is likely to waste everyone's time fiddling with the coffee maker, scrounging around for creamer, or popping out of the room to find a file or accept an interruption from a colleague. There's just something sacrosanct about staring into a monitor-mounted camera at a prearranged time.

Implement a zero-tolerance policy regarding scapegoating. The upside to teleworking is that distance workers largely get to stay out of the interoffice political stream. The downside is that they are at a disadvantage for defending themselves once they are sucked into that stream. Traitors are chicken. And it's so much easier to set up and blame the absent teammate they won't have to look in the eye. As a manager, it's your job to make sure that the team culture is one where everyone takes full responsibility for his or her own work and maybe just a little extra responsibility for each other's work.

Be sure to invite your teleworkers to real or virtual social events with your team. Even if your teleworkers are independent contractors, if they're regular contributors to your organization's efforts, don't overlook them when building your holiday party guest list. If they're full-time, permanent employees—just far-flung ones—make sure you have built into your budget travel funds to bring them to the office, ideally at least once a quarter. Four face-to-face meetings a year beat 15 daily interruptions.

Remember that teleworkers need to be engaged as much as their onsite colleagues do. They need your attention. They need to know that they have a key role in helping the organization achieve its objectives (and they need to know exactly what that role is). They need to be able to trust their coworkers. And they need to know and care about the intrinsic value of the company to the marketplace overall.

Teleworkers also need to know that there is forward momentum in their careers. Professional development is still an important engagement driver for your offsite employees. When you bring your telecommuting employees in for their regular onsite visits, be sure to reserve some of that time to focus on their career development needs and interests.

Whatever you do, lighten up on the IMs. Unless you know for an absolute fact that your teleworker loves interruptions, resist the urge to ping. Interruptions are interruptions—even if you've got this really funny thing to say.

TRUTH

64

Your team has untapped talent

You don't need to be a psychologist to know this principle about the way the brain works: You tend to notice most those things that are important to you. If you're looking for your door keys, you're not necessarily noticing that your cherished copy of *Sgt. Pepper's Lonely Hearts Club Band* is the fourth LP from the left on the shelf over the stereo. You *might* notice the dust bunny under the couch, but usually only if the keys happen to be embedded in it. You can sleep right through the siren on the street below your open window, but your child's sniffles will keep you awake all night. And if, after years of dreaming, you've finally resolved to buy that red Corvette, you're going to suddenly see a lot of red Corvettes on the road.

We notice what's important to us, a habit that can be traced back to the times we lived cheek-to-jowl with mastodons. We needed to pay attention to what was going on around us just to stay alive. And to help us out with this essential task, our brains learned to filter out the trivial details. We couldn't be so deeply distracted by watching the flitting of a moth that we didn't discern the faint shift of air on the back of our necks as a cheetah closed in to strike. We wouldn't have survived long enough as a species to invent that Corvette.

> We may be forfeiting a more empowered, inspiring future.

Today, thanks to the invention of such things as doors and fast cars, we can afford to relax and look around at more details that our brain would have earlier dismissed as unnecessary to survival. We have the luxury of seeing beyond what we *need* to notice what we actually *have* and how we might be able to use those attributes to make our lives even better.

We practice this same survival-level focus at work—especially when we consider who our employees are and what they can do for us. We may hire people specifically to help us with our core business survival needs. But, with that job-specific focus, we tend to overlook the other talents they bring to the team. Consequently, without meaning to, we may be forfeiting a more empowered, inspiring future for the sake of tackling the basic survival needs of today.

Even if you're still barely staggering along in survival mode, invest at least a couple of hours every week in exploring what else your team can bring to the organization. For starters, take a fresh look at their resumés. Remember that they were probably tweaked to respond specifically to the published requirements of the job your employees ultimately landed. A variety of talents and skills might have been edited out or thrown into the background to highlight those abilities and skills you had originally asked for.

Search the resumés and applications to discover what other talents and passions might be buried there. You may discover, for instance, that you have a cadre of multilingual employees who can use that untapped skill to open new markets in previously neglected communities or countries. Or perhaps one of your employees has special expertise, understanding, or personal contacts in a relatively unique market, but a market, all the same, that represents customers who could uniquely benefit from your product.

> All that passion, knowledge, and talent represent a resource that will open all sorts of doors of opportunity.

Likewise, make sure you keep up with your employees' ongoing development and education efforts, especially the classes they take independently, for the sheer love of learning. All that passion, knowledge, and talent that your employees voluntarily acquire after they have met their own survival needs represent a resource that will open all sorts of doors of opportunity—for your company, for your employees, and for you. All you have to do is just look up from your survival-level tasks and notice.

TRUTH

65

People need to fight their own battles

In the business world, people work in close quarters—even if they're half a globe apart. When limited resources (time, money, space, raw materials, personal imagination) clash with unlimited catalysts (personal agenda, grudges, mistrust, misunderstandings that travel the speed of the Internet), you've got yourself some trouble among the ranks. It's going to happen sooner or later. Prevention, of course, is almost always a good management approach. But no matter what you do to prevent the predictable conflicts, the unpredictable ones come up in their place. How you handle a conflict among employees is a hallmark of engaging management.

How you handle a conflict among employees is a hallmark of engaging management.

Handle it poorly, and you've got unresolved conflicts that could persist for years to come. Handle it well, and you've got an even tighter bond within your team of employees—even if they have to agree to disagree. If you're committed to empowering your employees to independently solve business problems without running to you for every decision, make the same commitment to empower them to solve their interpersonal problems equally independently. The agreement they strike—and own—together will be far more powerful than any solution you force on them just because you're the boss.

Take every grievance seriously. If your employee is peeved enough to come to you, that's reason enough for you to listen. Bear in mind, though, that you two have separate reasons for this initial conversation. His is to vent and then, perhaps, seek a solution. Yours is to assess. If you're hearing evidence of harassment, threats of physical violence, bullying, or substance abuse, this meeting needs to be documented and kicked straight to your legal or HR department. This one is out of your hands.

Even if complaints turn out to be laughably petty, don't belittle the employees—or their complaints—and then josh them on their way. Give them a serious and respectful hearing, without taking sides. It may feel like a waste of time at the moment, but you're building your own reputation as someone who cares enough to listen. The next beef might not be so trivial, and you want to know about that one, too.

Assuming that the complaint is relatively benign (something that won't require the services of your attorneys, the police, or paramedics), encourage them to resolve the dispute without your intervention. Presumably, everyone is a grown-up in your office. So make it clear you respect your employees enough to expect them to act like adults. Provide conflict resolution training once every year or so (even more frequently, if necessary, depending on your

You're building your own reputation as someone who cares enough to listen. The next beef might not be so trivial, and you want to know about that one, too.

new employee turnover or how emotionally charged your workplace is). This way, your employees will follow the same rules of the game. If, as a pair, two conflicting employees work on the mutual goal of achieving an agreement, relying on the same procedure they learned in the safe, hypothetical confines of a classroom, they will discover *together* that the system works. And you may have, as a result, a newly minted, freshly bonded team of two that you can then assign to a happier, more productive project.

Don't treat the conflict as a floor show. This is not a battle of impassioned titans who bring the spectacle to your office for your amusement. If the issue is serious enough for your employees to be upset about, it's serious enough for you to be respectful of.

If you must bring the antagonists into your office for a conversation, don't allow the exchange to disintegrate into a showdown. Make sure *you* are professionally trained in facilitation skills. Establish the ground rules up front that you are meeting to discuss behaviors and expectations—not personalities, bad breath, or body odor.

If the issue is serious enough for your employees to be upset about, it's serious enough for you to be respectful of.

Don't hold this episode against the vanquished. Employee conflicts should never be about who wins and who loses. They should always be about working toward an agreement and using the experience to build greater understanding and trust. If there is to be a loser in the conflicts among the people you manage, make sure that they lose just this battle, not their face, spirit, or heart.

TRUTH

66

Games don't build teams

Some people just don't like to be afraid. And some people really don't like to lose their composure, face, and bladder control while standing on one foot atop a telephone pole. And hearing "You can do it!" shouted encouragingly 30 feet below from one's coworkers doesn't help one tiny little bit.

Most team-building games, challenges, and events accomplish only one thing: They serve to remind us that despite outward appearance—and very real adult financial obligations—we really haven't made much progress in wisdom and perspective since we were 15. And neither, by the way, have any of those bullies and weasels who have also only gotten older and taller.

Those Outward Bound wannabe exercises such as ropewalks, rappelling, trust falls, and endurance hikes are fabulous confidence builders for people who are pretty confident already. They know that they're capable of doing so much more in their lives and jobs if they could only bust through some self-imposed boundaries and negative thinking. But no one should actually be *forced* to go through those experiences. Certainly not in front of people they have to see again, especially at work. At work, now as before, image is an essential component of our confidence kit. We like to keep our fears and any incompetence to ourselves:

> At work, image is an essential component of our confidence kit. We like to keep our fears and any incompetence to ourselves.

- ■ **Reserve what matters for what really matters.** When you're balancing on a single rope 50 feet from the ground, trussed in a cat's cradle of very intimate straps, and wearing a dumb-looking helmet, with all eyes on you from the ground, that rope matters a lot. But a week later, the only thing that remains is the humiliation. That's not helpful the next time you're presenting a $70 million merger proposal and you just know that those two snickering in the back of the room are saying, "Hey, you remember the time Bob peed his chinos on the ropewalk?" It's distracting, to say the least.

- ■ **Some people just have different ideas of what fun is.** Shared memories of pleasure are lovely bonding moments. The best ones, though, come from within the group, not from a

229

menu of prepackaged themed events that a consultant tells you will bring the most return on your investment. Casino nights can be fun, except for someone who needs to stay away from gaming tablesand doesn't particularly want you to know about that. Margarita nights can be a blast, with potential for some great pictures afterward, except for the person who needs to stay away from tequila (and who doesn't want you to know about that either). Forget about barbeques; you might have a stealth vegetarian onboard. Karaoke nights can be fun, except for the person who doesn't particularly want to look like an idiot. Anything after work can be a laugh riot, except for the people who have to get their kids from daycare.

See the problem here?

Any group experience should be toward reinforcing the pride, joy, trust, and respect among the team members so *everyone* can move forward with the confidence that his dignity is intact. There are plenty of bonding moments and chances for a good laugh as everyone pulls together on a shared vision of success. Ultimately, business results are what really matter.

The best team-building experiences in the world are the ones that allow passionate, dedicated, and talented people to get the chance to give their best toward a common goal. If you don't have that as part of your daily workplace culture, no expensive, high-risk experiential event is going to make that happen. If you do have that as part of your workplace culture, save your money.

> Business results are what really matter.
>
> The best team-building experiences in the world are the ones that allow passionate, dedicated, and talented people to get the chance to give their best toward a common goal.

The workplace world is rife with opportunities to experience fear and exhibit ridiculous behavior. Why pay for it?

The fun will come naturally.

TRUTH
67

Answers build teams

While it may be true that companies are built one hire at a time, teams within those companies are built by answers—answers that come via chunks of experience that demonstrate to employees in real-life terms that their efforts are well invested with their company. As we've already established, balancing on a telephone pole doesn't guarantee the formation of a team. But the day-to-day pulling together toward a common goal will. It just takes more time. And a whole lot of answers to core questions that drive trust and performance standards will build quality teams over time.

These are the questions that really influence your team-building exercise. It's not a matter of answering them "once and for all"—it's a matter of answering them over time through the decisions and choices you make as the team leader:

> Answers to core questions that drive trust and performance standards will build quality teams over time.

- Will we be working on challenging assignments that are meaningful to us, both personally and professionally?

- Will we agree with each other most of the time about what excellence looks like in our goals and our behaviors?

- Can I trust my teammates to have my best interests at heart?

- Will I consistently care about my teammates to make the necessary sacrifices and exert the extra effort toward our shared goal?

- Can we trust our manager to add only new hires to our team who share our standards of trustworthy, high-quality behaviors and performance accountability?

- Can I depend on my teammates to be accountable for their job responsibilities and actions?

- Will my teammates inspire me to perform at my very best levels— and hold me accountable for strong performance standards?

- Can I trust my teammates to be tolerant and supportive if I fall short of a commitment or standard of behavior?

- Can we trust our manager to provide us with everything we need to do our best work?

- Can I count on being able to keep learning and continuing my professional development?

Real team building is an emotional journey that you can't buy in a box or farm out to a consultant. It comes from a history of consistently kept commitments, shared goals met, standards enforced, and visions reignited with fresh passion and energy.

You're only human, and you're learning, too.

You have the power to build engaged teams motivated by trust and dedication to your mutual mission. No one is expecting you to have all of the answers all of the time. You're only human, and you're learning, too. But, as the engaged manager, you hold in your hands most of the right answers *over time*. And those answers will build the team of your dreams.

TRUTH

68

Your team can lead you to greatness

Probably one of the most enduring models of pre-engagement business cultures is the idea that leadership flows downward only. The longer you stick with this form of gravity-bound management, the longer you'll be enjoying only partial engagement. Engaged employees ready to take the lead on projects they own will chaff under old leadership styles. Let your people take the lead, and you'll be amazed at how far they'll take you on the strength of their own vision:

■ **Let them know you want to intentionally pass on some of the power.** Get their buy-in on this plan. But don't expect a unanimous approval. Some employees—no matter how self-directed they are, in fact—may be uncomfortable with the idea that the power will be disseminated throughout the team rather than concentrated with just you.

> Let your people take the lead, and you'll be amazed at how far they'll take you on the strength of their own vision.

■ **Brainstorm with your entire group on what shared leadership will look like in your team.** Will they have the latitude to tell each other what to do? Will they be individually responsible for making important presentations up the managerial food chain? Will you be comfortable letting your direct reports speak one on one with your boss and boss's boss without your being there?

■ **Find out what their personal hidden beliefs are about leadership and management.** Do they think of being the boss as a positive role? Or as a policing job? Or do they prefer leaders to be merely facilitators? Can they devise a set of values and expectations of what they want from someone who has the leadership role within the group? Can all members find a new, comfortable role for themselves in this new context—including those who prefer to simply report to you?

Identify what behaviors of your own you're going to have to change. As you transform your employees into leaders, you may have to get used to being a follower again. Can you tolerate that? You may have to get in the habit of giving them more information more quickly than you used to. They may expect you to explain yourself more now, when before all you had to say was "*Because I said so.*"

> ## You may have to get used to being a follower again.

- **Work with your team members to discover what additional training they need to exercise their new leadership responsibilities well.** Can you create a budget for courses on presentation techniques, having difficult conversations, using time effectively, etc.? Some courses, such as presentation skills, should be taught be experts. But you can also create a self-study program, such as a book club, to help your staff members build their competencies and understanding of what it takes to become true leaders as a journey of personal growth. Brown-bag lunch discussions of books they read as a group will help them see how this journey challenges their coworkers as well as themselves.

- **Learn to consider your team members as an advisory board.** Keep in mind that they are probably more expert in their particular field than you are. While they may still have more tactical-level responsibilities in your department, they can also lend their expertise to you and the group as a whole. This added perspective will give you the chance to see issues and concerns in fresh new ways—which will then ultimately help you make better decisions.

> ## They are probably more expert in their particular field than you are.

The German author and philosopher Johann Wolfgang von Goethe wrote, "Treat people as if they were what they ought to be, and you help them to become what they're capable of being." In the same light, treat people as if they are already the leaders they're capable of being, and they'll help you become the manager of a team of inspired change makers.

TRUTH

69

You're still the boss

Take a moment, if you will, to imagine the perfect day at work. By the time you arrive, everyone is already there. Everyone works brilliantly together. All your employees completely understand the many layers and values of pulling together as a team toward a common goal. They work long hours when necessary, without being told to. They support each other's efforts and celebrate each other's successes. They trust each other implicitly because they themselves are trustworthy.

All except one. And that's the one person who makes you doubt the entire construct of employee engagement and the power of intrinsic motivation. This is the person who challenges you every day to remember that you're still the boss.

It's one thing to consider the fine, most-elevated points of leadership and high-performance management in the safe confines of ideal-world thinking. But it's quite another thing to look at employee engagement from the battlefield perspective. And sometimes it is a battlefield. If it's been a rough quarter so far, you might be looking at a landscape pocked with the craters and smoking heaps of projects gone bad and rivers running red with the ink of failed, expensive initiatives. It could be one bad employee who has caused such devastation or the whole team that has set back the entire cause.

If you've been leading your department with the perfect-world ideals of engagement, you will have to make some tough decisions—and soon. Take a fresh look at your company's published, formal set of values. Consider how you can realign your own actions to both reflect those values and to use them as the leverage you need to assert your authority to drive performance to higher standards.

> Consider how you can realign your actions to reflect your company's values and use them to assert your authority to drive performance to higher standards.

- How can you use your company's culture of trust, caring, inspiration, belonging, and tradition of excellence to *influence* your people to perform at an elevated level?

- How can you use your own behaviors as a way to model the standards you want *all* your people to aspire to?

- Who can you reach up to in your organization for coaching and leadership support that will help you keep your team dedicated to achieving the goals you've set for yourselves but also the culture in which you want to achieve those goals?

- Do *you* need to be recommitted to the ideals behind your organization's mission?

- What training do *you* need to strengthen your ability to lead with both inspiration and authority?

However self-directed your team may be, you are still the leader. It's up to you to establish and model the ideals and principles of your organization in the way you run your group. Remember the principles of engagement that we established in the beginning of this book:

> **However self-directed your team may be, you are still the leader.**

- Engaged employees believe in the mission of their organization.

- Engaged employees love what they do and understand how their jobs serve the bigger picture.

- Engaged employees don't need discipline; they need clarity, communication, and consistency.

- Engaged employees augment their skill sets with positive attitudes, focus, will, enthusiasm, creativity, and endurance.

- Engaged employees can be trusted, and they trust each other.

- Engaged employees respect their managers.

- Engaged employees know that their managers respect them.

- Engaged employees are a constant source of great new ideas.

- Engaged employees will give you their best.

There's one more: Engaged employees know who's boss. That's you. And you owe it to your people to exercise your mandate to get results by tapping into their most dedicated passions and efforts.

> **Engaged employees know who's boss. That's you.**

It's your job to get the best from your people. When you do it well, your people get the best from you.

References

Truth 16

"Cultivating Positive Emotions to Optimize Health and Well-Being," by Barbara Fredrickson, *Prevention & Treatment*, Volume 3.

"Why It's So Hard to Be Fair," by Joel Brockner, *Harvard Business Review*, March 2006.

Truth 32

"It's Not a Fair Fight If You're the CEO," by Marshall Goldsmith, *Fast Company*, December 2004.

Truth 37

The Power of Appreciative Inquiry: A Practical Guide to Positive Change, by Diana Whitney and Amanda Trosten-Bloom, Berrett-Koehler Publishers, Inc., San Francisco, 2003.

Truth 42

"Let's Hear It for B Players," by Thomas J. DeLong and Vineeta Vijayaraghavan, *Harvard Business Review*, June 2003.

Truth 50

"Sparking Creativity at Ferrari," by Gardiner Morse, *Harvard Business Review*, April 2006.

"The Six Myths of Creativity," by Bill Breen, *Fast Company*, December 2004.

The Artist's Way, by Julia Cameron, Tarcher, New York, 1992.

Truth 51

"Organizational Creativity," by Wendy M. Williams and Lana T. Young, in *Handbook of Creativity*, edited by Robert J. Sternberg, Cambridge University Press, New York, 1999.

Truth 54

"The Six Myths of Creativity," by Bill Breen, *Fast Company*, December 2004.

Truth 55

"The Six Myths of Creativity," by Bill Breen, *Fast Company*, December 2004.

Creativity: Flow and the Psychology of Discovery and Invention, by Mihaly Csikszentmihalyi, Harper Collins, New York, 1996.

Truth 57

"Managing Your Boss," by John J. Gabarro and John P. Kotter. *Harvard Business Review Onpoint*, Executive Edition, Winter 2006.

Truth 68

Leadership from the Inside Out: Becoming a Leader for Life, by Kevin Cashman, Executive Excellence Publishing, Provo, Utah, 2000.

About the Author

Martha Finney is the creator of the Career Landscapes team-building workshop, and a management consultant specializing in helping companies identify and build passion-driven workplace cultures. She is also the author or coauthor of 18 books, including *HR from the Heart: Inspiring Stories and Strategies for Building the People Side of Great Business,* with Libby Sartain, former CHRO of Yahoo! and Southwest Airlines. Her clients and interviewees include executives from Intuit, the Central Intelligence Agency, Avery Dennison, The Gap, Inc., Starwood Hotels and Resorts, Caterpillar, Kenexa, and H-P.

Martha's work has been featured in major newspapers, including the *New York Times*, *Wall Street Journal*, and *San Jose Mercury News*, as well as in *Time* magazine and on CNN and NPR's Morning Edition. She is based in Santa Fe, New Mexico. She can be reached at Martha@marthafinney.com.

FINANCIAL TIMES

In an increasingly competitive world, it is quality
of thinking that gives an edge—an idea that opens new
doors, a technique that solves a problem, or an insight
that simply helps make sense of it all.

We work with leading authors in the various arenas
of business and finance to bring cutting-edge thinking
and best-learning practices to a global market.

It is our goal to create world-class print publications
and electronic products that give readers
knowledge and understanding that can then be
applied, whether studying or at work.

To find out more about our business
products, you can visit us at www.ftpress.com.